Presents

Donald Gorgon's

Cop Killer

Published by THE X PRESS, 55 BROADWAY MARKET, LONDON E8 4PH. TEL: 081 985 0797

Distributed by Turnaround, 27 Horsell Road, London N5 1XL
Tel: 071 609 7836

Printed by BPC Paperbacks Ltd, Aylesbury, Bucks.

This book is dedicated to M and ruffnecks everywhere.

ONE

The late August evening, hot and humid, brought the residents of Hackney out onto the streets in their scores. As darkness fell, Stoke Newington High Street bubbled with the rhythms, verbal exchanges and odours, of diverse slices of ethnic life as folk went about their business or simply chilled out on street corners taking in the breeze. It was a lazy evening. Outside the many Turkish cafes young men sat deliberating about their next move in a backgammon game, illuminated only by a street light. Along the High Street, designer jeeps and open-top sports cars cruised leisurely in the night traffic. Near to the Negril Caribbean Take-away, a group of hooded youths with half-eaten patties joked boisterously as the latest ragga tunes pumped from the stereo of a low-slung BMW convertible parked up on the kerbside beside them. Saturday night in the ghetto. All along the street, youthful Asian shopkeepers pulled down the shutters on their late-night grocery stores and shouted friendly greetings to each other, after another profitable day's work. In front of the pub on the corner of Church Street, two punkish-looking girls were drunk and engaged in a noisy impromptu karaoke. Nobody paid them any attention because the warm evening had brought out a trailer-load of modelling queens to brighten up the night and there was hardly room for a bad vibe anywhere.

The mood of the evening was distinctly carnival-like, with everyone enjoying the heat of the moment. In contrast, the atmosphere in the unmarked police car was tense and awkwardly silent. In the front passenger seat, the Detective Inspector mopped his brow for the umpteenth time. In the back, the two detective constables were in quiet contemplation. The Detective Sergeant at the wheel broke the silence.

"Come on you fuckin' coon, move that fuckin' motor!"

He flashed his headlights and the Ford in front pulled away from the green traffic light slowly, reluctantly, but not before its driver had slipped a piece of paper to the smiling girl standing at the crossing. As the burgundy Cavalier cruised up the High Road, the Sergeant vented his frustrations about the changing face of the neighbourhood.

"God, this place is looking more like fucking Istanbul every day. This used to be a really nice area, but I'm glad I don't live here anymore. It's a fucking rubbish tip. All the shit of the world comes here, from Pakistan, from Niggerstan and from Coon City. What a fuckin' mess, eh?"

A die-hard cockney, 36-year-old Detective Sergeant Keith Summers had served seventeen years in the Force, working his way up from pounding the beat to plain clothes and eventually being made a Detective Sergeant at the nearby Stamford Hill police station. He was about to further elaborate on what was wrong with the country when the Inspector cut in.

"Let me just go through the plan of action for this evening once more so we don't have any fuck ups. Okay?"

Inspector Martin Reid glanced at his watch. It was 10:35 pm.

"When we get to the address at Navarino Street, myself and Sergeant Summers will be first into the property, while you two cover our backs. Okay?" Seeking confirmation, he glanced over his shoulder at the two detectives in the back seat.

"No problem, Guv." replied the blonde-haired one.

2

The Inspector looked again at his watch.

"Keith, you're sure this tip is kosher?"

"Yeah Guv, I don't think that coon would dare to fuck me about. The cunt was shitting himself and the info he's given in the past has been legit," reassured the Sergeant.

"Never underestimate these fucking niggers," his superior cautioned.

Earlier on in the day the Inspector had obtained a magistrate's signature on a warrant, giving permission to search the Stoke Newington home of Phillip Baker on suspicion of supplying illegal drugs from that address. The information came from a Hackney-based small-time dealer, Michael Watts well-known to the officers. Sergeant Summers had stopped Watts' car in Stamford Hill early that morning and found £1,000 worth of cocaine hidden under the driver's seat. In return for letting him go, the Sergeant had demanded the names of other 'unofficial' dealers in the area. Baker's was the only name not known to Summers. After 'confiscating' the coke and £300 Watts had in a jacket pocket, the Sergeant warned him about operating on "my manor without a licence". He satisfied himself that Watts fully understood his drift before letting him go. Nothing could be allowed to upset the well-established understanding, between officers at Stamford Hill police station and local drugs dealers, that the cops would turn a blind eye to their activities in return for weekly 'operating fees'. Freelancers like Watts, trying to operate outside of the system, would not be tolerated.

Michael Watts sped away, grateful for the lucky break. Any other time he would have been riled about losing the stash and the money, but he had only just completed a stretch at her majesty's pleasure anyway. The policeman wanted names; Watts gave him some, but the officer wasn't satisfied. For some reason, someone he had known back in his school days in Stokey came to him. In his desperation to avoid another spell in the cooler himself, Watts volunteered the guy's name. It didn't matter that Phillip Baker had no involvement in the local drugs scene, as long as it got this policeman off his back.

Now, four armed officers were heading for Navarino Street, with the intention of converting another freelance dealer to join the 'system'. With the local yardies' penchant for 9mm 'matics, the police had no intention of making a house call without their own hardware, just in case Phillip Baker fancied himself as a baby gangster.

The Cavalier turned left off the High Road down Manor Road. Summers pressed the accelerator hard and the speedo touched 50 down the wide, tree-lined road.

"Take it easy Keith, I don't wanna end up in Homerton Hospital tonight," the nervous Inspector warned.

He looked at his watch.

At 43-years-old, the Inspector no longer had the stamina or enthusiasm for the job. He would happily leave The Met but huge debts caused by the collapse of his brother-in-law's printing business, where he was a sleeping partner, meant he was desperate for money and therefore took an active role in the rife corruption at Stamford Hill.

The Inspector's stomach felt unsettled and he was still sweating profusely. He mopped his brow again. The possibility that in five minutes he could be involved in a shootout with a yardie made him tense. With the growing number of attacks on officers, he was only too aware that these days being a policeman carried no special dispensation from a yard man's 'matic or a cockney's sawn-off. He leant his head nearer to the open car window to catch some cooling breeze and patted the butt of his .38 revolver, reassuringly in its leather holster. He could feel the weight of the pistol strapped to his waist, but needed to confirm with his hand that it was still there. He looked at his watch. It was 10:45.

The Cavalier took a right into Navarino Street. As it slowly drove down the quiet road, the Inspector peered out trying to make out the house numbers.

"Number 72. That's it, that's it. Pull over behind that Granada," he instructed.

A small, tree-lined road of modest, late-Victorian terraced houses, Navarino Street was like others of its type in Stoke Newington and elsewhere in London. There was nothing of note about number 72 or the adjoining houses. A small, front, brick wall was topped with ornamental concrete blocks. The old sash windows had been replaced with double glazing. The curtains were closed and there appeared to be no lights on in the house.

In the car, the yellow glow of an overhead street light illuminated the Sergeant's face, giving it a sinister appearance. A middle-aged man walking a dog stared suspiciously at the car and its passengers as he went by. The Sergeant held the man's stare until the dog walker turned his head and kept walking.

"Well, we'll soon find out if anyone's at home, eh Guv? The coon's probably shagging some slag in there," the Sergeant said with a grin.

"Okay let's go to it. Put your hats and armbands on," the Inspector instructed. "And remember, there's no reason to shoot unless you get beef."

Dressed in jeans, T-shirts and trainers, their crew-cuts and regimented appearances were dead giveaways to the casual observer, quite apart from the baseball caps and armbands marked 'POLICE' — which in the heat of action ensured there were no misunderstandings.

The officers alighted from the car and waited by the metal gate at number 72. The Sergeant joined the other officers, having removed a large sledge hammer from the boot of the car. Despite their warrant, it was generally accepted in drugs cases that a polite knock on the door by the police gave a dealer all the time he needed to dispose of the merchandise. There was only one way to catch a pusher, the Sergeant knew, and that was the tried and tested 'element of surprise'. He quietly opened the gate and moved quickly to the front door. Immediately behind him was the Inspector with his .38 Smith & Wesson in his right hand. The two other detectives had also drawn their revolvers. The Sergeant awaited his cue from the Inspector.

"Is everybody ready?" the Inspector asked tense.

"I'm as ready as I'll ever be," the Sergeant answered equally hyped up and feeling for his gun. He was half-hoping the black bastard would make a run for it.

"Okay, lets go."

With the wooden shaft of the sledge hammer gripped firmly in both hands, the Sergeant lifted it above his head and brought it down with all his might on the Yale lock. There was a loud smash and and a cracking of wood but the door held its ground. The Sergeant quickly raised the hammer again and once more brought it down with force. This time the Yale lock shattered and the officers threw their weight behind the door. They only managed to open it a few inches, however. A security chain still blocked their entry. As more hammer blows rained down, the Inspector gripped his gun tightly in his sweating hand. The chain was evidence that someone was at home.

The door finally gave way. The Sergeant dropped the sledge hammer and stepped aside. Seized with panic, the events that followed were a blur for the Inspector. He was the first into the house which was in darkness, apart from the street light outside illuminating the first few feet of the hallway. Dizzy with a rush of adrenaline, his left hand, fumbled, trying to locate a light switch, as his heart beat to the point of bursting. A warning flashed through his mind and he hesitated. Suddenly, there in front of him on the stairs, he could just make out the shape of what he thought was a man pointing a large silver handgun. The

6

Inspector raised his gun and shot twice, his eyes shut tight in a mixture of fright and anticipation. The hallway was momentarily lit up by a flash of flame from the muzzle of his Smith & Wesson, then there was a thudding sound as the body fell limply down the stairs.

With her legs twisted on the last three steps and her torso facing upwards, lay the body of an elderly black woman. Her face lay to one side, opened eyes frozen on a vacant expression, her left hand trapped behind her back. Her white night dress turned slowly red as blood oozed from a large chest wound. In one clenched fist she held a silver candlestick holder...

That night Verone Baker had said a little prayer before closing her Bible and preparing for bed. It was a nightly ritual, one she repeated alone since the death of her husband, in the solitude of a bedroom echoing with memories. The brown-skinned woman, her face a thousand wrinkles and her head full of grey hair, had barely laid down to sleep when the deafening crash downstairs shattered her peace. She was sure the commotion must have come from outside, but decided to go down and check that everything was as it should be anyway. But then came the voices, the shouting, the orders. She only just managed to reach for a dressing gown from the wardrobe, realising now that something was seriously wrong.

She hadn't heard the sound of the policeman's gun before she was thrown off her feet by a bullet exploding into her chest and she fell to the ground...

For a few moments there was no movement from any of the officers. The Sergeant realised he had to act fast. Pointing to the blonde-haired detective, he ordered him to find a towel to stop the bleeding. He instructed another

7

detective to go to the car and radio for an ambulance. He then tried in vain to find a pulse on the elderly woman's wrist.

"Fuck. I think this one's a gonner," was the Sergeants' verdict

The Inspector was waking from his daze.

"Oh my God. Oh my God. I'm going to be in the fucking shit for this, Keith. The fucking shit. I could have sworn it was a fucking bloke with a gun. Jesus Christ!"

The Inspector was in big trouble and he knew it. How would he explain that it was either him or her? That these raids were a question of survival and he had to move fast to stay alive.

As the Inspector talked, the Sergeants' mind was already trying to put the pieces together.

"Listen Guv, let me have a word." Summers headed towards the door of the lounge. The Inspector followed. The lounge was immaculately decorated. In the bay of the window was a large television set and video. A plush-looking green dralon settee and two armchairs took up the space along the length of one wall. On the other wall was a fireplace with family photographs and souvenirs from Jamaica and Barbados on the mantlepiece.

"Guv, this ain't a fucking good situation to be in, but I think there are a couple of ways we can save our bacon. You know what I think?"

There was silence. The Inspector stood beside the fireplace, deep in thought, as he studied a photograph on the mantlepiece of a couple and two young boys.

"That fucking black bitch, Keith. My career will be fucked because of this. Fucking ruined... Sorry Keith, what were you saying?"

"Guv, I've still got that gear I took off Watts. I think I'd better leave it here just in case the forensic boys from the Yard don't find anything else. You would be totally shafted if you shot some old darkie and there was no evidence of any dealing going on from this address."

"Yeah, yeah that's good thinking, Keith. Make sure your prints are wiped from the packet. Leave it in one of the bedrooms."

The Inspector was waking from his initial state of shock. He didn't intend to be sent down for this cock up. His survival instincts had told him to be concerned with saving his own arse, not the woman he had just shot.

The Sergeant rushed out of the lounge, up the stairs and into the first bedroom he came to. He opened the top drawer of a black-finished chest of drawers and took out a sock. He used it to carefully wipe his fingerprints from the small self-seal style polythene packet containing the cocaine he had confiscated from Michael Watts. He then dropped the packet into the sock and replaced it carefully in the drawer.

As he walked back down the stairs, the ambulance crew was arriving outside. Residents had gathered in front of the house and the rumour that police had shot their neighbour was clearly audible, as it circulated amongst them. The blonde-haired detective constable and his colleague were on 'sentry' duty outside the house, keeping the agitated and growing crowd at bay. The detective took a handkerchief to his brow and wiped the sweat. Even though he was dressed in plain clothes, his stature, bull neck and bow legs gave him away to the local inhabitants as a cop. It made him nervous.

A white woman in her early forties shook her head as tears streamed down her cheeks. She stood in only a dressing gown and pink slippers, glaring at the blood on the blonde detective's T shirt.

"God, what have you done to Mrs Baker, you murdering bastards?!" she shouted. Her Irish accented voice was shrill and close to hysterical.

Already the news was spreading like wildfire from one flat to another and eventually even to other black areas in the city. It was hot news.

In the hallway of number 72 Navarino Street, the body of Verone Emily Baker, aged 57, born in the parish of St Ann, Jamaica, mother of Phillip and Lloyd Baker, was being lifted onto a stretcher.

At 11:54pm at Homerton General Hospital, Verone Baker was officially certified dead. Cause of death was a gunshot wound to the heart.

TWO

The traffic on the approach to the Blackwall Tunnel was solid and barely moving. A long snake of red brake lights disappeared into the distance. Frustrated commuters on their way home to the suburbs tried flexing between the three lanes of the motorway in the vain hope that there would be some magical way out of this. There wasn't. This was 5:30pm, rush hour, and the worst possible time of the day to drive from Bow on the north side of the river, to New Cross in the south.

As there were no bridges east of the City, motorists relied on one of two tunnels to drive across the river. The Blackwall Tunnel was the heavyweight however, with a motorway on either side to service it. On the north side, the motorway sliced through a once close-knit working class community. The residents of Bow to the West and Stratford to the East rarely crossed the high-speed divide to each others' neighbourhoods. A view of the motorway with its six lanes of speeding traffic in both directions was now the only thing they had in common.

The raw, unadulterated sound of hardcore rap and ragga boomed from the minicab's speakers; the radio tuned as always to the militant sounds of Ruffneck FM. Some called it a pirate and some called it an illegal broadcaster; to its thousands of listeners, Ruffneck was 'The Voice of Hackney':

"I'm a gangsta fanatic

Shoot any fucker trying to cause some static
I heard shots, two three, four, five, six
Then I saw brothers pumping their motherfucking fists."

Lloyd Baker kissed his teeth as another car cut in front of him, advanced a hundred feet, then moved back into the inside lane. He reached inside the pocket of his leather jacket and took out a packet of cigarettes. In the back, his passenger was becoming irritated with the wait. Lloyd looked in the rear view mirror and saw the impatience on her face. She was an attractive woman of dark complexion, wearing leggings and a brightly patterned blouse. As she looked from side to side at the packed rows of cars, her large dollar sign gold ear-rings reflected the summer evening's sun. She reminded Lloyd of his ex-girlfriend, Sonia, and his mind drifted off.

"Cho' man, this is pure road block. I'm supposed to be picking my daughter up at 6:00pm. Ain't there no other way to get to New Cross?" The woman's shrill cockney - patois cut Lloyd's reminiscences short.

"You got a helicopter? Nuh worry yuhself, man. Relax!" Lloyd said wryly. To anyone who travelled the streets of London as often as he did, the best way to get through a traffic jam was not to think about it. "Time longer than rope, man," he concluded, "so learn to have patience.'"

Dollar Gal was in no mood for philosophy lessons.

"Is it?" came her curt, sulky, disinterested reply.

Lloyd lit his cigarette and surveyed the urban wasteland, which the locals called 'Siberia', bordering the motorway on both sides. The Eastway which serviced the tunnel, had been planned to cut right through the middle of a no-man's land between Hackney and Stratford. The high-rise residential blocks which dotted the landscape in the distance looked bleak, facing a backdrop of traffic-jammed bumper to bumper and engulfed in a smog of carbon monoxide exhaust fumes. Most of the commuters stuck in the peak time traffic felt themselves fortunate for having somewhere better to live than the immediate surroundings. The taxi driver scratched his goatee beard as his mind wondered off again. He thought about the time he and his brother Phillip had taken their mum out on a surprise trip to the theatre up West, for her birthday. They went and saw *Carmen* — which she had always wanted to see. Lloyd remembered vividly the three of them walking happily through Piccadilly Circus after the show and going for a meal in Soho. It was the first time in all her years in England that their mum had dined at a West End restaurant and she had been excited about the whole event.

The blaring horn from the car behind jolted Lloyd back to the present. He slipped the Ford Sierra into gear and drove two hundred yards to catch up with the tail of the traffic jam.

It took another 35 minutes to reach New Cross and he was glad Dollar Gal was the last fare for the day. As he headed back towards Blackheath and the northbound tunnel entrance, Lloyd radioed to inform Sanjay, the boss of the mini-cab firm, that he was done for the day. His return journey was relatively quick. Back in Bow, Lloyd took a pit stop at the local off-licence for a six-pack of Tennants before heading to his yard.

Lately he had been drinking heavily to help him sleep nights. For the first six months after his mother's death he had been like a duppy: the living dead, quietly suffering the slings and arrows of outrageous fortune. He still had problems sleeping, but at least the alcohol numbed the brain and eased the pain. And when he wasn't drinking, he burned the sensi, anything to avoid facing the cold and empty reality of life sober. Maybe he was losing a grip on things, he couldn't remember the last time a day passed without him ending up wrecked. And today was no different. He hadn't planned any special moves tonight, so like last night and the night before, and the night before that one, he would retreat to his flat, get drunk, fall asleep on the sofa and hope he could stay asleep until six in the morning when his day would begin again. Never having had a telephone, he didn't miss it. And although he would regularly big up a handful of familiar faces, he never gave out his address. He no longer went out raving and wasn't too concerned whether he pulled women now and then or not. He lived a life too private to accommodate the stress of a relationship.

He turned into Michael Connoly Gardens and parked the Sierra in the communal parking area. He disconnected his mini-cab radio ariel and stored it in the boot, then headed towards the stairs. Michael Connoly Gardens was one of the better council estates in Bow. The well-maintained, low-level council blocks were seventies-built, and unlike the earlier sixties-built monstrosities surrounding the Estate, were well liked and looked after by their inhabitants. The June evening was warm and bright and as he made his way across the car park, Lloyd encountered several of his neighbours setting forth for an evening out.

"Lloydie, wha' ah gwan, boss?"

He turned to see the familiar smiling face of a dread he knew. Patrick was a neighbour, and a mechanic Lloyd had sometimes used. As always he was dressed in his 'regimental' baggy ragga jeans and a green string vest. The two men touched fists in mutual respect.

"Yeah Patrick, long time. Ah wha' yuh ah seh, enh? Where you been at, man?"

"Well stranger, is I who should ask you that," the dread replied, jokingly pointing a finger. "Well me lion, is over a year now, boss. I know seh t'ings been rough fe yuh, Lloydie. Bwoy, me sorry fe hear 'bout your mother still... Is pure fuckries going on for black people in this

14

country, you know. I only jus' reach back from J.A after almost a year, y'know. I jus' couldn't believe it when my bredrin told me about yuh mother."

The two men exchanged a few words. Patrick could see that Lloyd didn't really want to talk about his family's tragedy and excused himself after some minutes, explaining that he was late for a meeting with his cousin. Lloyd continued through the communal entrance to his block and walked up the stairs to the third floor. The tremendous public sympathy for him and his brother since their mother's death always made him uncomfortable. On the one hand he was grateful for all the kindness, but on the other he didn't know how to explain to people that discussing her death was still too painful for him. It was ten months since her death, yet it only seemed like yesterday. Only in the last two months had he managed to comprehend the fullness of what happened. Before that he had been gripped by shell-shock and ran on auto pilot, but the reality was now dawning.

He closed the front door behind him and stepped into the living room where he hit the button on the stereo, filling the room with the high decibel sounds of Ruffneck FM, the most popular of the pirate radio stations broadcasting reggae daily across north-east London. From the bathroom, where Lloyd had gone to take a leak and to hold a fresh, the lyrics of the song blasting from he stereo were barely audible, but the persistent, insistent ragga beat was unmistakable. Lloyd recognised it as the rhythm to a successful deejay tune bemoaning the violent deaths of too many Jamaican artists, and hummed along from memory:

"Same way dem kill Big John, Fluxy an' Echo,
And make Prince Far I's woman a widow
Same way dem kill Peter Tosh, Free I an' Tubby,
Next t'ing me know dem find Tenor Saw in a gully

Lee Van Cliff he died as a crackhead
Dirtsman dem shot him up inna him bed
Carly Barratt get full-up ah lead
Mikey Smith get stoned till him drop down dead
Same way dem kill Major Worries,
Same way dem kill Hugh Mundell
That's why I sleep with my .44
'Cause I can't trust crowd ah people no more..."

As he washed his face , Lloyd glanced at himself in the mirror above the wash basin. He was looking older than his 27 years. The months of little sleep, excessive stress and Tennants Extra had taken their toll. There were bags under his constantly bloodshot eyes and the wrinkles across his forehead gave him a permanent frown. He was a stone lighter in weight, which for a man who had always been of slim build, was a huge discount, and it had caused him to stoop slightly at the shoulders. His unkempt hair needed trimming bad and he had recently found a few strands of grey hair in his goatee beard. He dried his face then looked in the mirror again. He sighed and pulled out the plug.

In contrast to his rough appearance, Lloyd's flat was extremely neat and tidy, to the point of being unnaturally sterile. The position of the two loudspeakers had been measured precisely to achieve the optimum stereo effect. His records were catalogued in alphabetical order and as with the perfectly-aligned books, there were just as many records as there was space on the shelf for them. The furnishings were minimal and of varying styles and revealed few clues about the tenant. An old vinyl sofa draped with an Indian-style bed cover provided the room's main seating. By the wide sliding windows which ran the length of one wall, were a couple of cheap, three-shelf white bookcases containing a wide variety of crime fiction, from Victor Headley's *Yardie* trilogy to *The*

16

Godfather. There were a number of conscious books also such as *Roots* and *The Autobiography of Malcolm X*. Next to the bookshelves was a TV, video and basic hi-fi. Along another wall was a small table with an angle poise lamp. Two chairs accompanied the table. There were only two items on the walls: a poster of two touching black fists advertising Victor Headley's bestseller, *Excess*, and a cork notice board covered with layers of newspaper cuttings about the shooting of Verone Baker. A cutting with the headline: 'MURDER CHARGE COP WALKS FREE' was pinned to the centre of the board; a constant reminder of the pain he had endured and the pain he did not want to forget. A gun target sight had been drawn carefully and purposefully in red felt pen over the face of the police Inspector who had shot his mother, pictured walking from the Old Bailey with his wife.

Lloyd returned from the kitchen after leaving some beers in the fridge to cool. He sank into the sofa and pulled the ring off a can of Tennants. A refreshing breeze wafted through the open window, gently rustling the yellowing cuttings on the notice board. The loud knock at the door made him jump.

Lloyd opened the front door to find his brother standing on the step. From the unsmiling look on Phillip's face it was obvious that this was going to be one of those 'serious talking' sessions.

"Phillip, yeah man, come in." Lloyd touched his brother's fist with his own, playfully, and opened the door wide for him to enter then followed him through. "I wasn't expecting anyone, but that's safe. You want a Tennants?"

Phillip Baker observed his older brother closely but said nothing. Lloyd sensed the bad vibe immediately.

"Look, Phillip man, I've been meaning to phone you. It's just that I've been under pressure."

The younger brother tried to remain calm but couldn't

maintain his cool.

"Fuck that shit man!" His usual black cockney accent slipped with ease and volume into patois as he became more angry. "Cho' man. Yuh t'ink seh you is the only man under pressure? Fuck that! T'ings still haffe run, y'know. Here I am trying to sort out family business yet me don't get no rahtid support from you. Yuh t'ink seh t'ings easy fe me? Fuck that, man!"

Lloyd thought it wise to let his brother get the anger off his chest and decided to say nothing until the initial storm had died down. Phillip had always been extrovert and emotional, unlike his brother who tended as a child to be quiet and introspective. Even at school where he became known as a 'loner', Lloyd spent playtimes by himself, locked in his own thoughts, seemingly unconcerned about peer group pressure. Phillip had grown accustomed to his brother's ways. Their mother's death should have brought them closer together, but strangely their relationship had strained, as each man struggled to come to terms with their loss in his own way. Lloyd handed his brother a Tennants from the fridge and waited for the right moment.

"Phillip, jus' cool, nuh man. What you're saying is right. It's been three months since I saw you and I know that's bad. I got your messages but things got on top of me and you know how it is when I'm under pressure, I ain't no use to no-one."

Phillip Baker sipped from his can while studying the newspaper cuttings on his brother's notice board.

"You know, I didn't even see all these articles when they were printed," he said. "What you got them up for? I don't know how you can wake up to them every morning."

Phillip cracked a bitter smile when he saw the makeshift gun sight drawn carefully over the Inspector's head.

"Shooting's too good for that mother fucker. If there's a God, that cunt's raas will burn in hell."

"Don't worry Phillip, judgement day haffe come," Lloyd began. He remembered how it had pained his brother to see his mother's killers placed on suspension after the shooting. In Phillip's view, 'suspension' was police doublespeak meaning a vacation for services rendered.

"You don't really think they're going to get away with it, do you? In this world there's justice and there's righteous justice. Nuh worry yuhself, bro, every dog has his day—some sooner than others. When I think of Mama and how kind and gentle she was, it's like her memory won't let me feel any hate against those cops. But the other night while I was driving around everything became so clear Phillip, and I got to understand that what goes around definitely comes around again. Maybe today, maybe tomorrow, but it definitely coming around, yuh dig wha' me ah seh? And since then, I ain't had no strong memory of Mama. Yuh see wha' me ah show you, bro?"

Phillip turned around. The tired look in Lloyd's face, the loss of weight and his uncombed hair worried him. No, he didn't understand and considered instead how the strain of their mother's death was taking its toll on his brother's mental health. He walked over and put a hand on Lloyd's shoulder.

"Listen, I'm sorry. I don't want to cause no bad vibes between us. Let's sit down and reason things through."

London's black community had reacted strongly to the killing of Verone Baker. Realising that he had a potential riot situation on his hands, the Metropolitan Police Commissioner suspended all the officers involved and charged the Inspector with murder. Three months later an inquest returned a verdict of 'unlawful killing' over the death of Mrs Baker.

There were violent scenes outside the Old Bailey when

a jury cleared the Inspector. The defence had claimed it was a terrible accident and that the police were risking their lives every time they raided the property of "a yardie drugs dealer" and that they had to be extra vigilant. The cocaine found at the Baker household helped to convince the jury that the police followed guidelines for dealing with a "dangerous drugs raid." The unspoken verdict of judge and jurors was that Mrs Baker's death was the tragic consequence of her son's drug offences.

No charges were ever brought against Phillip Baker as there was insufficient evidence to prove that he knew the cocaine was in the house or that he was connected with it. A month after his acquittal at the Old Bailey, the Inspector took early retirement from the Met.

Lloyd returned from the kitchen with another two cans of Tennants.

"The Met are going to settle out of court for damages," his brother informed him. "They have put forward £300,000 which our solicitor says we should accept. What d'you think?"

"Phillip, whatever you think is right is sweet with me." The look of anguish on Lloyd's face suggested that his mind wasn't on what his brother was saying. "All I know is that all the money in the world ain't going to bring Mama back. When they murdered her they may as well have put a gun to my head and pulled the trigger, because from that moment time stopped for me and since then life has been one long road of pain..."

The brothers exchanged a knowing look. They both still hurt from not having their mother around.

"Fe real," sighed Phillip.

Even though he was only 23, Phillip Baker had been forced to take on the maturity of a man above his years. He had become a self-trained legal expert — dealing with the claim against the police, the sale of their mother's house; being a media spokesman on behalf of 'The Justice for Verone Baker Campaign Group', whilst also trying to hold on to his sanity and keep up with his college work at the LSE where he was studying accountancy.

The two brothers sat and talked for a couple of hours about the financial arrangements. Phillip spoke of the word that the Sergeant involved in the death of their mother was still in the Force and had been transferred to another station; that their solicitor was looking into the possibility of taking out a civil prosecution against the Inspector and that there were plans for a 'Black Rights' demonstration.

"I'm going to try and meet up with Hackney's black MP Erskine Pinnock later on this week to see what he thinks about the demonstration," explained Phillip, eager to involve his brother in the campaign. "What do you think?"

Lloyd was standing by the open window staring out at the fast-moving cars rushing along the nearby Blackwall Tunnel motorway.

"Yeah Phillip, that sounds like a good idea."

His reply sounded disinterested, Lloyd marvelled at his younger brother's diligence and stamina. Phillip had fought the good fight against their mother's killers, even though the chances of a conviction were remote. The ten month struggle seemed to Lloyd, at times, longer than a marathon, but he had to hand it to Phillip for never running out of steam.

Phillip wasn't convinced of the sincerity of Lloyd's reply. "Look man, jus' speak your mind if you're not happy 'bout things," he said earnestly.

Lloyd avoided distressing his brother further by sounding more positive this time.

"No seriously, I think its a good idea. Fe real." He paused, then spoke again. "But to tell you the truth, I don't think anything will come of it, because there ain't no justice for black people in this country. I read a line in a

21

book which said, ' 'justice' is the means by which established injustices are sanctioned'. Ain't that the fucking truth, bro?" He was staring at nothing in particular now, and the roar of the traffic on the motorway outside drowned out many of the words. "All over the world people talking about 'peace an' love' an' 'throw down the alms house business'... 'Peace an' love'? But I don't want no peace an' love an' there ain't ever gonna be no peace until we get equal rights an' justice — all over, in Africa, in America and right yahso! Especially yahso! Without justice, the only peace they've got for us is 'rest in fuckin' peace... or rest in fuckin' pieces. "

The sound of motor cars tearing down the motorway outside filled the void left by the two brothers' prolonged silence. Finally, Phillip decided that nothing more productive could be achieved at this meeting and began to make his move. He finished his Tennants and got up to leave.

Lloyd had moved from the window and was now examining his notice board.

"You met that reporter from The Inquirer, Jackie Spencer, what was she like?"

"Yeah, she's done some good articles on the Campaign," Phillip replied. She seems genuine, you know, very keen. Why do you ask?"

Lloyd removed an article from the board written by Jackie Spencer and handed it to his brother.'ANGUISH OF COP VICTIM'S SON' was an article about Phillip Baker and was dated three months after the shooting.

"This article she wrote was safe, y'know. She really expressed what we went through. Like she really understands."

Phillip looked uneasily at his brother then down at the article.

"Yeah sure, it was a good article... Listen, I've got runnings to sort out so I'd better start making tracks. I'm probably going to J.A. with Sharron for a few weeks, just to chill out a bit, in a couple of weeks, but I should see you before I go. Let's not leave it three months again, yeah?"

They walked to the front door. Phillip stepped out, then almost as an afterthought stopped and turned to hug his brother.

"Lloyd, look after yourself bro. Try and get away for a break somewhere. You won't believe the good it can do you to chill out up country for a few days We're all that's left of the family now so we gotta hang tight, yeah?"

Lloyd smiled. "Don't worry about me lickle breddah. Babylon cyaan keep a good man down. I'll keep in touch. Respeck." He touched fists with his brother and said his goodbyes.

Alone once more, Lloyd finished the last can of Tennants, turned up the music and rolled an ital spliff without tobacco. His head still spinning from the lethal mixture of sensi and brew, he danced around the flat with his knees dipped slightly and his fingers cocked up in the air to simulate pistols. He danced over to the photograph of the police Inspector on his notice board and took careful aim down the sight. He fired both his 'guns' and with a smile of satisfaction blew the imaginary smoke from the 'barrels' and then went to lay down to sleep on the sofa...

In his four years as a mini-cab driver Lloyd had carried some strange fares and requests and this was beginning to seem like one of them. He had clocked on at 7:00am and this was his first fare of the day. He suspected that the passenger was going to be trouble the moment the guy stepped in through the door of the mini-cab office on the Bow Road, but agreed to drive him nevertheless.

The man was of medium height but very strongly

built; a white man in his mid-forties with short hair and heavily tattooed arms. The shellsuit pants, baggy T shirt, bum bag slung around his waist and gold chain around his neck gave him the appearance of a market stall holder.

"Oi, gunga din. I want a car to Woodford," was his opening remark to Sanjay, the cab firm's owner.

Lloyd drove the man to his destination and parked outside a modern block of privately owned flats. His passenger was not ready to alight however, and simply sat in the car staring up at the windows of a flat in the block. Despite the early hour, 'Cockney Wanker' smelt strongly of alcohol and was clearly on an angry vibe in the back seat of the Sierra. They had been sitting in the car at a standstill for five minutes and Lloyd's patience was wearing uncharacteristically thin.

"Listen mate, I can't wait here all day. You only told me that you wanted a cab to Woodford. If you want to sit in the car you've got to pay."

'Cockney Wanker' reached into his pocket, pulled out a £20 note and threw it into the front.

"There ya go, san. Now shut ya maff."

Lloyd turned the volume up on his car stereo, lit a cigarette and kept quiet. He occasionally picked up passengers who had nothing better to do and nobody else to fuck with than a cab driver. Right now though, he wasn't in the mood for being fucked around.

"Where's the volume on your fuckin' radio, eh? Turn the fuckin' fing up some more...! That fuckin' slag, she must fink I'm a right cunt. I know she's fuckin' some geezer in there. Well she's got another fuckin' fing coming."

'Cockney Wanker' took out a small whiskey bottle from his trouser pockets and emptied its remaining contents into his mouth. "Listen san, I don't fuck abou' when it comes to someone tryin' to take me f'a twat. You know wha' ah mean? Ah've got a fuckin' shotgun in doors, san. Y'ever seen what a shotgun can do t'a bitch's cunt, 'ave ya? I'll fuckin' stick it up 'er cunt. Fuckin' slag."

Lloyd's patience had finally come to an end.

"Cho', come out me car, man. I don't need to listen to this foolishness first thing in the morning. Tek your money and come out of me car!" He turned around to hand the man his money but 'Cockney Wanker' had other ideas.

"Fuck you, sambo. I'm payin' you for y'time so shut ya maff and do as ya told."

Lloyd had heard enough. 'Cockney Wanker' was full of himself but the alcohol had clearly deadened his reflexes. Before he realised what was happening, the taxi driver's fist had smashed into the bloke's nose with a sickening crunch. By the time the watering of his eyes had subsided enough for him to see, he was being dragged by a now bloodied T Shirt out of the rear passenger door. 'Wanker' made a wild swing with his left fist, but it failed to make contact. Instead, he ended up with his cheek grazing the road, and felt the brunt of the taxi-driver's anger as a combination of kicks and boxes rained down on him. 'Cockney Wanker' yelled in pain as blow after blow struck his head. In the haze, he caught glimpses of the black high-top training shoe as it steadied itself to take aim, but each strike came with such rapidity and deadly accuracy that he was powerless to resist.

Lloyd pulled the limp body of the man from the road and propped him up against the side of a parked car. He didn't know what came over him and had been unable to check his fury. The man shouldn't have tried to test him. A stream of early morning rush hour traffic passed by, but the motorists had better things to do than to stop and get involved. Blood trickled freely down the man's nose onto his light-blue now torn T-shirt. His face had already swelled with bruises. Despite the severity of his beating 'Cockney Wanker' was still defiant.

"You fuckin' nigga, I'll fuckin' kill ya! I'll fuckin' get ya! Fuckin' nigga you're a fuckin' dead man!!"

Lloyd kissed his teeth, got into the Sierra and headed back to Bow...

Even at 10:00am the traffic on the Whitechapel Road was slow moving. The area which was once a bustling business area had declined into little more than a thoroughfare. It had begun to resemble a depressing, urban hinterland of dead, grey streets, abandoned shops and warehouses and lifeless tenements. Lloyd was surprised at how the violence he had dished out in the incident earlier in the morning, had had little effect on him. He had to admit that he didn't care whether the bloke was alright or not. Insults had become almost routine in the job, but the taxi driver refused to tolerate them. He regretted cleaning the blood off the seats, he should have made the bloke get down on his knees and lick it up.

His thoughts drifted back to the other evening with Phillip. He was proud of the way his kid brother had come though all of this tragedy. Phillip seemed to be coping and the strain didn't appear to be affecting his studies. It was ironic though that the person who would have enjoyed seeing him graduate the most, the person Phillip devoted his studies to, wouldn't be around to see him complete them. Mama had so looked forward to seeing her son become an accountant.

Phillip had always been the academic one of the two. It wasn't that his older brother wasn't able, but when their father, Cecil Baker, died of lung cancer when Lloyd was thirteen, he lost interest in a lot of things — including school work. His father's death affected him as it would any loving son. They were very close. From an early age Lloyd had shown interest in the electrical engineering his father had spent his life engaged in and Mr Baker was only too glad to impart all his knowledge to his eldest boy. When other young boys were playing with Action Men and train sets, Lloyd learned how a radio worked and what the main components of a television were. He had only fond memories of his childhood and his one regret was that his father's dream of one day retiring to his native Barbados with his Jamaican wife Verone, was another dream that would never materialise.

His father's death was a blow to Lloyd so strong that he still wasn't sure he was over it fully. He had changed from being a shy but happy child, to one who was moody, introspective and disinterested in everything around him. He left school at sixteen to work in a factory in Islington, but he quickly got tired of the job and after picking up his first wage packet, walked out the gates and kept on walking... He drifted from one dead-end job to another — labourer, packer, cleaner and courier — and went from one brief relationship to an even briefer one. Nothing seemed permanent in his life, least of all an address and by the time he moved into his hard-to-let flat overlooking the motorway, he had experienced temporary residence in most of London's inner city boroughs. He finally settled on becoming a mini-cab driver; a job he liked because it gave him a chance to be in his own world with no boss breathing down his neck all the time. When he didn't feel like talking he only had to turn the radio up loud to keep his thoughts to himself and the thoughts of others locked out.

He was now driving south over Tower Bridge and had already forgotten the last ten minutes of his journey from the Whitechapel Hospital. Lloyd was on his way to Camberwell to drop off a young woman passenger and her child. As always when he crossed the river, he felt like

27

he was entering an independent state with its own customs and distinct dialect. Although the taxi driver's native east London still had some of the vilest poverty and slum residences in the country, somehow south London always seemed depressing seen through the eyes of a north Londoner. He turned and offered the woman a cigarette and lit one for himself then tuned the radio into Ruffneck FM:

"Yeah, respect to the massive, to the maximum, every hour on the hour from the control tower. Yes nice and decent people throughout the capital, some serious tunes haffe drop on the turntable this morning, yuh know. Alongside the roughneck deejay soldier General Culcha. Strickly revival business we ah deal wid an' who don't like it can gwan an' lef' yah. Coming your way, the legendary Mr Big Yout', the musical entertainer from Kingston, Jah-maica. Watch the ride..."

The tune brought memories flooding back to Lloyd, sweet memories of teenage days in the blues dances around Hackney and Stokey, back in the days when raving really was *raving*. Big Youth's music had been influential in his life and most recently had brought him and his last serious girlfriend, Sonia, together. He remembered vividly how they got chatting about a track on the tape he was playing when he drove her from Clapton to Forest Gate in his cab.

"Sky juice — the sufferer's style. You know this tune did really big up the ghetto people's side of things when I was living in Jamaica," Sonia had commented from the back seat. "Because in those days poor children couldn't afford coca-cola and had to settle for sucking from a cellophane bag on a piece of ice with flavouring — sky juice. And on the record Big Yout' is saying that is a good thing because it means that the sufferer man could earn a raise by selling sky juice from his barrow, and then circulating that money in the community. Otherwise the money just disappears to America when we buy the bottle of coca-cola."

Lloyd was impressed with the reasoning of this obviously conscious black woman. It had never occurred to him that the song had a deeper level which he had missed altogether. He warmed to her easily. She seemed to like him also and agreed to meet up the next day.

The relationship, his longest, lasted two years before Sonia reached exasperation point and could take Lloyd's lack of emotion and his long hours of silent introspection, no more. Lloyd sensed she was unhappy long before the relationship ended. He had a soft spot for her, but found himself unable to make the effort to improve. He couldn't even talk to her frankly and admit that he was tired of sex with her and wanted to be on his own.

All that had been eighteen months ago, and apart from the occasional 'lickle t'ing' there had been no one special in his life since. Lloyd envied his brother who on the other hand had a good relationship with his woman, Sharron, and was even considering marriage.

"Stop, stop it's just here luv."

The woman passenger was worried that the cab driver had forgotten her destination and would drive right through Camberwell. Lloyd's reflexes were sharp, however and he swung the car expertly into a space and pulled up by the kerbside. The woman paid her fare hurriedly and climbed out. Lloyd spun a U-turn and headed to Brixton to score some herb.

'Downtown' Brixton resembled a neighbourhood in New York City rather than south London. It now boasted to be the black capital of London, which was the black capital of Britain, which was the black Capital of Europe. The area now contained a multi-complex cinema, a string of upwardly-mobile buppie shops, and the largest Caribbean-style market for a thousand miles in any direction. This battle-scarred area of London and its long-standing Caribbean community had overcome all adversity to become a bustling, thriving, booming happy neighbourhood, with a rastaman's shop on every other corner; blasting the latest reggae tunes through mega-speakers and where you were never more than twenty yards away from a pattie. Recently, a new breed of black businessman/woman had moved into the cheap, ex-frontline stores, offering a more varied and better quality product than the traditional businesses. This new breed looked professional. They had their shopfronts painted in the most elegant colours and revived the ethic that 'the customer is always right'. They ran barber saloons where the hairdressers were creative artists with a razor, haute cuisine restaurants with uniformed staff and well-stocked bookshops because they always paid their invoices and on time. These traders were well-respected and attracted increasing numbers of shoppers from outside the area. Most of the black communities in the country were represented on the High Street as Lloyd drove along slowly, because everyone knew that 'Brixton run t'ings'. Nowadays white shoppers flocked to the place also, reassured that the area was no longer a threat. After all, 'Brixton Riot' was now the name of a rum cocktail in a buppie winebar across the road from the tube station.

The traffic on Acre Lane was slow moving and his car was stationary for a time outside the offices of The Inquirer. Lloyd gazed across the road at the 1930's-style building that was home to 'Britain's Big, Broad & Black Newspaper' and wondered if Jackie Spencer was at that very moment writing an article that would destroy the lies surrounding his mother's death. No, that would be too easy. Only in films did the guilty get punished and the innocent rewarded. Real life was more complex than that, he thought. In real life, it was hard to separate the saints from the sinners. Lloyd drove on to his destination.

With his car parked at the kerb, Lloyd waited patiently outside the house. He rang the doorbell again and heard the sliding of a sash window above him. Trinity Gardens was one of those rapidly-becoming-gentrified streets off Acre Lane. The terraced houses were neatly painted and their trendy venetian blinds and stripped-pine front doors suggested that the residents were middle class lefties. Some of the traditional black inhabitants of the street had cashed in on the rising property prices of the 80's and had since moved on. Mikey, or 'Herbsman' as he was known locally, had spent all his life in Brixton and was staying put. His house was the last black outpost in this new yuppie frontier. He often insisted that he would neither retreat nor surrender and had painted the window frames and front door in striking red, yellow and green paint to make his point.

"Yo, boss! Mr Eastender! Yuh brave fe come visit dis yah parts, y'know!" Herbsman laughed from the upstairs window.

The front door opened and a gold ringed fist appeared from behind the door.

"Touch me, boss," said Herbsman as the two knocked fists.

A tall, red-skinned man in his early thirties, Herbsman dressed in a style more suited to the local youth than a man of his years. A short hair cut with an excessive amount of patterned tram lines and ragga-style dark glasses were his hall marks. That and the black and yellow 'Michigan' style suit adorned with an abundance of gold chains, gave the impression that he was someone who was particular about his appearance.

"Step forward yout'," He beckoned to Lloyd, who entered, closing the door behind him.

"Respeck Mikey. Long time, innit?"

31

"Fe true, 'iya. So wha'ppen; yuh get tired of that inferior East End ganja? You come fe check out the real yard sensi, ain't it?"

They both laughed. It had always been difficult to find the best herb over the river and Lloyd had to concede that with the recent saturation of crack on the market it was now almost impossible to find anything but the basic bush herb. After a month smoking some inferior weed from a white dealer he knew, he was now more than ready for a taste of the good stuff. As everyone knew, south London was the ganja capital of Britain and increasingly larger numbers of north Londoners were now prepared to make the trek down to Brixton and Peckham every Friday night to collect their weekly stash.

Lloyd sat on the black leather sofa in the front room while Herbsman weighed an ounce of tightly-packed prime sensi. He handed the taxi driver a plastic bag stuffed with the pungent herb and, as an afterthought, added a red packet of king size rizlas.

"You want a dragon, Lloydie?"

Lloyd set to work building a fat, conical spliff, while Herbsman popped the caps on two bottles of stout. The dealer watched the taxi driver shape a spliff expertly with the skins. He had watched people build up a thousand times and still couldn't resist the magic of the art. He took a swig from his bottle and leant forward to speak.

"People 'round here vexed about the court case, yah know." Herbsman fixed his friend a momentary gaze and then lowered his voice conspiratorially. "No way that Inspector should have got off, man. Yuh nuh see wha' me ah show you? Inglan' is renk, we're living in babylon. White man don't have no respect fe black people... No respect for our mothers. Something's gotta be done, man."

Herbsman drank his stout and waited for Lloyd's reaction. The taxi driver finished building his spliff impassively. He lit it and took a long, deep, contemplative pull that seemed to go on for ever. He felt the effects of the high almost immediately and kicked back relaxed, waiting to exhale the thick, white ganja smoke which eventually, engulfed the room in a cloud that hung around the light bulb. His eyes were bloodshot, but a peaceful calm possessed him. He pushed the stash over to Herbsman to build one up for himself

"I saw my brother Phillip last night," Lloyd said finally, "I tried to tell him wha' ah really gwan but I don't think he understood. You see Mikey, you have two kindsa people in this world, fucked-up rich white people and the rest who get harassed like us. And two kindsa justice: the court's justice — which won't let you do nothing about your harassment, and street justice. Outta street every dog has his day, yah dig wha' me ah seh?"

Herbsman knew exactly what he was saying. Like Lloyd, he was a man with little to lose. He grew up with police brutality common in his neighbourhood, where every day a young black man was arrested. Eventually they came for him.

"Me hear you loud an' clear, boss," Herbsman replied. " 'Cause me get lick from an early age, y'know, and I got to understand what they really think about us. All they do is tes' us. They just want the excuse to shoot us, an' when dem cyaan fill yuh up ah lead dem get you anudda way, seen? That's why they put crack in our communities in the first place, 'cause to them a 'dead nigger' is one problem less. But dem youts ain't stupid. Black youts play ruff, to survive. The cops got guns, but we got guns too. The only time dem respeck we, is when they're staring down the barrel of a Smith & Wesson... 'Boom, boom!' "

Lloyd listened patiently as Herbsman reasoned his point. Finally, he finished his drink and said he would have to go back to work. He handed Herbsman the money for the weed, but it was declined.

"Next time you can come back and buy a couple of

ounces!" Herbsman joked as Lloyd made his way out.

The rest of the afternoon was busy with several short-hop journeys. Lloyd checked off at 7:00pm, his head still buzzing gently under the effect of Herbsman's sensi. It seemed like the day had gone on for ever.

Back at his yard, he built up a killer spliff and enjoyed it, while watching the evening traffic from his open lounge window. He then surveyed the room to see if anything needed sorting. As ever, everything was tidy and in its place. His obsession for neatness had been passed down from his father who was always fond of saying that 'Order is heaven's first law'. When he was alive, Cecil Baker often summoned up the wrath of God on anyone who moved his tools from their correct place.

One spliff followed another and the room filled with smoke as the taxi driver flicked through the pages of the old family album. The faded photos of his newly-wed parents on their arrival in England in the fifties, looking strong, healthy, beautiful and hopeful, made his heart twinge. He turned to the photos of the young family; he in his shorts as a child and his mother carrying baby Phillip. Then photos from their school-days and extended family photos at ceremonies and parties, as one relative after another either married or christened their new babies. Then he turned to the later photos of Mama after she became a widow. The contrast with the earlier photographs was huge. She had aged greatly over the years of struggle to single-handedly provide a fulfiling life for her sons. A tear came to the taxi driver's eye as he considered that he never had the chance to realise the dream of sending his mother home to Jamaica in retirement, while he supported her in England

He pulled on the spliff again. The weed was much stronger than his usual stuff and once again Lloyd would start a new day by rising fully-dressed from his sofa early the next morning.

THREE

E vening was ticking close to night and the curtains in
many of the houses were being drawn. At number
52 a man sat reading a newspaper in an armchair at
the back of the room. The curtains remained open and the
light from the standard lamp near the armchair made the
seat's occupant clearly visible to any casual observer out
in the street.

A smart, red-bricked, Edwardian semi-detached,
number 52 was a typical residence in the leafy,
respectable streets of Wanstead. The house looked neat,
pleasant and far way away from the grey, motorway-
fringed high-rise tower blocks of Bow. Lloyd pulled hard
on the spliff until its tip glowed a bright orange. He lay
his head on the seat's headrest and blew a dense cloud of
white smoke. The cassette in the car's player was turned
down low, but just loud enough to make out the pulsing
bass line of a wicked dancehall re-mix.

He turned his head to look again. At the window a
man was drawing the curtains, a man who one night — a
year ago — prematurely extinguished the life of an
innocent black mother. Lloyd studied his face hard for the
brief moment it appeared at the window. The taxi driver's
insides twisted with hate and his eyes saw malice. Why
should this man live when Mama was dead?

At 9:30 pm sharp the front door opened and former
police Inspector Martin Reid jogged off down the road in
a blue vest and tracksuit trousers. Reid was a creature of
habit who clearly liked to keep in shape. For the third
time in a week, Lloyd kept surveillance outside the Reid
house. He wasn't sure why he was there. It was the first

anniversary of his mother's death and he had visited her grave earlier on in the week. That night, a strange dream had come to him. He saw himself armed with a sword, wading through a killing field crawling with snakes that sprouted in their hundreds from the mouths and ears and eyes of the dead bodies. Lloyd swung tirelessly with his sword, cutting off the heads of scores of snakes until he collapsed in a deep sleep, exhausted, unable to do more. After what seemed like hours, he woke to find himself still in the field, surrounded by the carcasses of the dead bodies. Fortunately the snakes were all gone and Lloyd went on his way through a field of skeletons. After what seemed like several days walking, he finally came to a house where he rested for the night. He awoke in the middle of the night, feeling the desperate need to go to the toilet. Even before he could climb out of his bed, he felt his bowels relaxing and to his shock he felt the warm and wet sensation ooze out of him as he messed in his trousers. When he looked however, a snake nestled in the seat of his trousers and another one was coming out of his behind. Lloyd screamed like crazy as he pulled the second snake out in a panic and then the third and the fourth. They just kept on coming, out of his behind, out of his mouth, out of his ears...

The dream seemed so real it shook him up badly and he awoke dripping with cold sweat. He had barely slept the last week and was so terrified of the dream coming back that he took to working day and night shifts.

He turned the key in the ignition, switched on the headlights and headed in the direction of Leytonstone High Road. The streets were busy with summer evening traffic. He wound his window all the way down and rested his elbow on the window frame. The stereo was turned up loud and there was still a glimmer of life in the spliff as it made its way down to the cigarette-packet roach.

36

"Girl tell girl and the rumour haffe spread...bad, bad and a wicked ina bed," the lyrics blasted from the tape.

The traffic lights changed to red and he pulled up in the nearside lane. He had just stubbed out the last of the spliff in the car's ashtray when the crackle of a police radio caught his attention. He turned to his right and saw a Rover patrol car in the outside lane. The vehicle's four officers were staring intently at his Sierra, not inquisitively but challengingly, daring him to make a move. Lloyd returned and held the stare. His eyes locked on those of the fat one with the red face, sitting in the front passenger seat, over-paid, over-fed and overweight. The officer's face seemed to grow a deeper red and from the contorted look around his mouth, he was clearly getting annoyed with the feisty driver's condescending stare.

As the lights turned to green the taxi driver knew he'd have to pay the price for his 'insolence'. His old Ford didn't have the speed to outrun the cops or he might have considered giving them a run for their money. The police car remained stationary and Lloyd pulled away, waiting for the inevitable. He had only travelled about 100 yards before the police car appeared right up his arse with siren blaring, blue lights on and headlights flashing. Lloyd drove on to the next junction and looked in the mirror again. This time they were bumper to bumper. He finally pulled over and waited. The policemen jumped out of their car and walked up to him slowly.

The fat cop was the first to the Sierra's driver's door. The sound of loud ragga music filled the air from Lloyd's car stereo.

"Turn that music off and step out of the car!"

You could tell from the tone in his voice that the officer wasn't about to take shit from anybody. He was ready for the taxi driver.

Lloyd, was in the mood for sport. He spoke in an

37

exaggerated cockney accent and held a cupped hand to his right ear.

"What ya say, mate? I can't 'ear ya the music's too loud."

The cop angrily leant into the car and turned off the cassette.

"I said get out! I'm not asking you again. Get out of the fuckin' car!"

The taxi driver slowly undid his seat belt and opened the door and climbed out. Fixing the heavyweight officer with a stare, he stood eyeball to eyeball, toe to toe.

"What the hell did you pull me over for?" he demanded with authority

"Just step the fuck back and shut up!" the fat cop barked, clearly in no mood for games. "Just keep your mouth shut or I'll give you something to complain about."

Lloyd casually leant against the rear passenger door with his arms folded. There was an urge to kill, to hurt and to maim inside of him, but he knew this wasn't the time to play his card. They were testing him. One wrong move and he'd be spending the night in a cell.

The other officers began checking over the vehicle, hoping they could find a bald tyre, an out of date tax disc or an inoperative windscreen washer. The fat cop searched inside the vehicle, hoping that he'd find stolen property, or maybe evidence of some dealing. Maybe he'd get lucky and find the product — a ki of top grade cocaine. They found nothing and fell silent for a moment, wondering what to do with their prey. When they finally spoke it was to each other in whispers, their eyes fixed on the young, black motorist.

As far as Lloyd was concerned, they were going through the formalities. As a young black man he had grown accustomed to the 'pull over to the side' routine. He had been down this road so many times he simply went through the motions, with his mind on other things. He was thinking of police and the power invested in

38

them. The smell of the power that these men held over every black man in their presence was awesome. Off duty, the brothers could make these guys cross over to the other side of the road, or lock themselves inside their expensive houses, too afraid to go out. But in uniform, they served the big pay-back. Fuck the fucking police, Lloyd thought to himself. They just couldn't handle the fact that things had changed, that the streets of London now belonged to black youth —spiritually, culturally and socially. As for the officers, they saw a potential 'yardie' in every black face and that had taught them respect they didn't want to show.

The fat cop couldn't miss the cold smile on the black man's face. He wanted to ask the driver what his problem was, but Lloyd's eyes told him, 'See, I don't give a fuck, that's the problem'.

After radioing in to check his driver's license the fat cop threw it into the open window of the Sierra. The cop issued him with a producer, clearly angry that they had found nothing to do the black man on. Fortunately for Lloyd, the half-smoked spliff in the ashtray had been missed when they searched through the car.

The cop's parting shot was predictable to him.

"You've been lucky son, just watch that attitude of yours. And if anything happens around here tonight, you're nicked."

The cop walked back to his patrol car but stopped suddenly in his tracks. He turned and stared at the taxi driver — his face a boiling red colour, like a freshly cooked lobster. He hadn't caught all the words but he had clearly heard the black driver say 'renk' and was familiar enough with Jamaican patois to know what it meant.

"What did you say son?"

It was not an enquiry, but a challenge to the black man to repeat himself.

Lloyd shrugged his shoulders, smiled and pointed to the bingo venue across the road. The word 'RANK' was brightly illuminated. The cop was lost for words and stormed back to the patrol car which soon sped off with him inside. As the back of the cop car disappeared down the road, Lloyd made his right hand into the shape of a gun and aimed it at the car.

"Boo-yakka! Every dog has his day," he said out loud, a grin stretched across his face.

As he continued on his journey back to the mini-cab office on the Bow Road, he thought about the number of times he had been pulled over by the radics. Things had cooled off a little, but back in his teenage years 'stop and harass' was routine police policy with black men. Lloyd recalled an occasion when, as a boy, he was with his father on a car journey from Sheperd's Bush to Ilford late one night. They were stopped by different police officers no fewer than five times on that journey, for no reason.

What he hated most about the almost daily pulls in those days was not the harassment or the waste of time, but the gawping white faces from the windows of passing cars. Those people who would think: 'Oh look another nig nog up to no good. If they weren't all villains, the police wouldn't stop 'em, stands t'reason dunnit?' To the average member of the public who never got that harassment, there was no other logical conclusion to come to. And who could blame them? Who feels it knows it, thought Lloyd.

The office of Swift Cabs was quiet this Thursday night. The yellow flashing light outside and its proud boast on the fading sign that 'No One's Quicker' seemed to be doing little to attract trade. Tunde, one of the firm's many Nigerian drivers, was reading a newspaper in one of the battered armchairs in the decrepit, glass-fronted premises. Two other driver's were playing a game of cards on the top of a Calor gas heater, which in winter provided the office's only source of heating. The red lino flooring was littered with dog ends and had clearly not been swept for some time.

A crudely constructed wooden partition wall separated the office in the rear from the front 'customer reception' area where the drivers sat on orange plastic chairs waiting for trade. A two foot square area had been cut from from the partition and the hole had been partly glazed and protected by a wire grill. Behind the grill the controller sat taking telephone bookings, dealing with the customers off the street, then relaying the information to the drivers via their radios or by shouting through the grill to the armchair drivers.

Tonight, Swift Car's main controller Millie was on duty. A large, brown-skinned, Jamaican woman in her late forties, Millie had a fearsome reputation for not taking any foolishness and ruled the drivers with a rod of iron. Sarcasm was her favoured weapon.

"So Mr Baker, yuh now reach. It was good of you to tek time out to pay us a visit. Fortunately we nuh busy now. It's a real shame when the customers come in and disturb we, enh?"

Lloyd wasn't in the mood for Millie's wit this evening and didn't want to get involved in a war of words.

"Yeah I'm sorry. I got pulled by the police up in Leytonstone."

"Is it?" replied Millie, clearly disinterested in any excuses.

He thought it best not to pursue that matter and sat down and lit a cigarette. By the time Lloyd had smoked it down to the filter the office was empty of all other drivers and Millie's booming voice was telling him the next job's address...

He blasted the horn again. Out of the darkness and into the the beams of the car's headlights came the figure of a young woman, half-walking, half-jogging, and trying not to stumble in her black suede platform shoes. Lloyd

41

caught sight of her — illuminated only for a brief moment — and liked what he saw: the white denim batty riders and the shapely legs in them.

She opened the front passenger door and jumped in. She was an attractive woman who could have passed for being in her early twenties, but on closer examination, Lloyd realised she was much younger: probably sixteen or seventeen. Still, she appeared to have the most stunning body. Her long, shapely legs complimented the slim waist. Her skin was of a dark brown complexion and seemed silky smooth. Under her tight, black, ribbed top the fullness of her breasts was clearly visible. A long black weave that ran past her shoulders and carefully applied make up gave her the appearance of a pop singer. She certainly looked fit. He tried not to stare at her legs as she sat down, but he couldn't resist. Their eyes met and he looked away, slightly embarrassed. She smiled.

"Don't worry big man, it don't hurt to look." She was clearly pleased with his uncomfortableness. Her cockney accent, made her sound white and older.

Joyner Gardens was one of the high-rise tower blocks that surrounded his estate and Lloyd was familiar with most of the residents. He had definitely never seen her before and she didn't quite look like a local.

"Dulwich. Which part?" he enquired.

"If you drive to the High Street I'll show you from there."

She rummaged through her small black handbag and examined the contents of her purse.

"How much will it be?"

"About ten quid."

"TEN pounds!" Her voice rose an octave.

"Dulwich is far, you know. You all right for the money?"

Lloyd was concerned that she was going to be one of those girls who were always trying to pull a skank. Apart

42

from robbery, assault, police, and accidents the biggest hassle facing mini cab drivers was the punter who didn't have the cash at the end of the journey. The freeloader knew that there was nothing the driver could do about it. You couldn't drive them back to where you picked them up and there was no point in going to the nearest police station. Skanks were an occupational hazard, and one that seemed to becoming more common place.

The girl in the batty riders was keen to reassure the taxi driver, especially as the Sierra was slowing down.

"Oh, it's no problem about the money; it's just that a tenner seems a lot," she smiled, crossing her legs awkwardly. "You been cabbing long?"

"About three years now. It's okay, but you've got to like driving and not mind working any hours. It's all the same to me."

She leant slightly closer towards him.

"And what does your girlfriend think about you working at night then? Don't she mind?"

Lloyd felt slightly uncomfortable. He didn't like being asked personal questions. What's more he was embarrassed that his answer might make him sound like a maama man.

'Well er, er... I don't really have... Well I'm not kinda in a serious situation right now. I'm kinda waiting for sump'n special to happen. You know what I'm saying?"

"Oh yeah. That's the way it goes. I've been seeing this guy and he's getting seriously out of order. One of these blokes who doesn't know how to treat a woman like a lady. He thinks he does, but he hasn't got a clue."

The conversation continued on that tip for most of the journey. Lloyd found out that she had been visiting a friend in Bow to help do her hair. She lived in Dulwich, and was unemployed. She said she was 20; Lloyd reserved his judgement. Her body said she was older, but her eyes told a different story. She said she wanted to be a dancer and could do a wicked bogle. Her name was Chantelle and she frequented the Barley Prince winebar on Peckham Rye. It was amazing how you could learn so much about a person in one cab journey, Lloyd thought to himself.

Lloyd turned the Sierra into upmarket Dulwich. He looked out of the window at the smart Victorian houses and wondered how she could afford to live there.

"Bumbaclaat! Ah your yard dis?"

"Yeah," she replied "It's a housing association place so the rent's cheap, innit?"

She looked in her purse.

"Listen, come in and have a coffee. I've left me cash indoors. I'll only be a minute."

She could see from his face that he was pissed off.

"Look, don't worry, I've got the money inside."

He sighed and reluctantly followed her up the short flight of stairs into the front door of the house. In the hallway, she opened the door to flat 'B'. It was nicely decorated and furnished in soft pastel colours but the chaotic state of affairs caused him to cast a disapproving eye. The lounge was cluttered with clothes. A plate with a half-eaten slice of toast sat on the carpet near the television and magazines were tossed liberally on the floor and the furniture. She invited him to sit down and Lloyd sank his full weight into the peach-coloured sofa. She offered him a coffee and disappeared to the kitchen to fix it.

Lloyd was starting to feel stressed. He didn't have time for this, but the girl seemed to be in no hurry to pay him. She returned with the coffee and disappeared out of the lounge for the money. When she returned a few minutes later she was laughing.

"You're not going to like this," she said giggling, "but I don't seem to have any money." She laughed some more.

The taxi driver kissed his teeth and got up vexed.

"This ain't no joke business, woman. Just go fetch my money."

By this time she had started to peel off her top and was unzipping her batty riders.

Lloyd was not expecting the move, and for the moment was frozen speechless on the spot, unsure of what was going down. His eyes fixed on her ample, yet youthful, breasts. He was unable to hide the surprise on his face.

"As I don't have the cash I thought we could come to some other arrangement," she smiled.

Lloyd laughed. He understood what the girl was saying, but he didn't take her seriously.

"Yeah, maybe later dahling, maybe next year. Because right now all I see is that you've got 'possible jail-bait' written all over you."

Lloyd looked her up and down and laughed some more, then added as an afterthought, nodding at her crutch, "Tell me, has it got any hairs on it?"

It was a good jest and Lloyd laughed uncontrollably. The girl didn't find anything to laugh about.

"I don't see no jail bait," she said, pushing out her chest to emphasise the point.

Before he could think or say anything in reply, she was removing his leather jacket and undoing the belt of his jeans. By the time the head of his cock was in her mouth he knew any objection was futile. His body would not allow it.

Months of sexual recession had weakened Lloyd's resistance. He felt a desperate frenzy take over him like a shark sensing blood. He slipped his hand under her batty rider and felt around.

"Is it hairy enough for you?" she asked with a 'told you so' look on her face. Lloyd didn't have to answer because his manhood said it all. She slowly unzipped the shorts to reveal the neatly, shaved outline of her pubic hairs. Lloyd didn't have to be coaxed further. He tore off his trainers frantically and fought to get his jeans off. His erection was so stiff that he thought his cock would burst as his hands wandered across the curves of her body. His left hand squeezed her buttocks playfully, while his right hand gently squeezed her ample breasts. He brought his mouth down onto her erect, right nipple and sucked hard. This was his show, he remembered, he was paying for it and he intended to enjoy it.

"Pull those batty riders down," he ordered, like he had seen the pimps do dozens of times in the movies. The girl obeyed him without protestation.

"I'm going to give you the best ride you've ever had," she assured him. "I'm sorry about the cab fare, but never mind; what's between my legs is sweeter than money, trust me."

"Just spread your legs," Lloyd ordered her. He had to take control of the pussy fast before she talked him out of time. As far as he was concerned, if he wasn't getting paid, he owned this pussy until he was good and done and he could do without the chit chat. He ordered the girl to kneel down and suck his dick again. She performed the task like a woman many years her senior and Lloyd's manhood stood firm like a rammer. He was ready.

The next moment she was lying on the floor and he was on his knees. He didn't see where the condom came from but she was now expertly unrolling it down the length of his wood. Then she spread her legs slightly as he let himself down on her. He could feel the warmth of her pussy at the tip of his cock, then he was enveloped by the warmth. She raised her legs around his back and he rode hard like a champion jockey, moving swiftly, expertly and firmly between her legs, as her loud moaning spurred him on. He knew he was too sexed to keep up the ride much longer and felt a hot rush drawing up from inside him. With a tightening of his buttocks he shot his seed and let out a moan like a man punched in the stomach. They lay still for a moment, their naked

46

bodies entangled with each other, then he felt his ardour rising again.

It was strictly cabin stabbing for the remainder of the night. The taxi driver called Millie at the office to explain that his car had broken down and that he would be out of action for the night.

Lloyd felt like a thirsty man who had not tasted water for a long time. He lapped up his nourishment greedily and eventually quenched his thirst. But first they tried and enjoyed it every which way and no position was left unturned. Lloyd was exhausted but satisfied. He had enjoyed himself to the maximum, especially when the pussy went snap, crackle and pop.

Hours later Chantelle shook him vigorously out of his post-coital slumber.

"Come on big man, you better make a move. My boyfriend's going to be back from work soon."

He didn't believe her as he hadn't seen any male possessions in the flat, but he didn't have much choice. He washed and got dressed. He asked for her telephone number. When she told him "I ain't got no phone," he got the message. He had noticed the phone in the hallway when he came in. He didn't feel a way about it however, it was a pleasant excursion and sweet while it lasted.

It was four o'clock when he climbed into his car. It was not long till daybreak and he had some serious business to sort out that day.

FOUR

His hand was shaking and try as he might he couldn't keep the razor still. He was tired, but couldn't sleep and had forgotten when he last slept peacefully. Now when he looked in the mirror, he was confronted by a haggard face older than he remembered it. Weary with fatigue, his eyes were swollen and the pupils danced around their sockets restlessly. Lloyd abandoned his attempt at shaving and wiped the foam off his face. He went and sat down on the sofa and lit the half-smoked spliff from the ash tray.

He had'nt intended to fall asleep on his return from Dulwich; there seemed little point as he needed to work the shift that day, but he lay on the bed for a moment and fell into a deep sleep. He had woken with a bolt, covered in sweat and shaking. The dream had haunted his sleep again but this time the ending was different. He was still walking through a misty green field and the contorted bodies of the dead were still there. Even the purple snakes which pushed their heads through the rotting flesh of the dead were there. He was still frantically severing the heads of the beasts with a large silver sword. This time in the dream, when he tried to rest because snake-slaying was thirsty work, one of the bodies got up and started walking towards him. It was too far away to make out the features of the person but as it got closer he could just make out that it was a black man. And gradually, as it got closer, he could see that it was his father. He carried a polished knife in an outstretched hand and told his son to get up and finish his task.

The dream had seemed so real that he was still unsure

whether it was a dream or if it really did happen. He just couldn't decide. Was it a message from his father? If it was, it wasn't the first.

The slam of the letter-box flap made his heart beat faster. He breathed out slowly, trying to calm his nerves, then rested the spliff in the ashtray and walked to the door.

'FEELING IRIE' was the inscription on the front, with a photo of palmtrees at sunset. The postcard from Jamaica was from his brother, who apologised for not getting together before he left, and said that he wanted to spend more time out there than he'd originally intended. It was signed 'Nuff Respect, Phillip'.

Lloyd's mind wondered back to his meeting with Phillip all those weeks ago. All the talk of compensation. From the police!! It wasn't Phillip's fault that he wasn't militant. Lloyd pinned the postcard on the notice board. He looked at the article by Jackie Spencer. 'ANGUISH OF COP VICTIM'S SON'. He wondered if she of all people saw things as they really were? Maybe she understood...

At each of the twenty or so desks in the long, rectangular, eighties-style, yuppiefied office, journalists were busily tapping the key boards on their Apple Macintosh computers, rushing to meet a deadline. The light grey walls complemented the light grey desks on which sat light grey computers. A long glass wall of metal-framed windows stood clothed in yards of grey venetian blinds. Originally designed and built as a factory, the spacious flat-roofed 1930's building on Brixton's Acre Lane was now home to 'Britain's Big, Broad & Black Newspaper'. Housed in the top floor of the art deco-style building, The Inquirer was a long established 'stepping stone' for some of the country's most talented black journalists, hungry for their big break to big fame and big money on the nationals.

It was 10:30 am and the day was already in full swing in The Inquirer's editorial offices. Jackie Spencer was keen as ever to get the scoop over her fellow journalists. She sat with the phone hooked under her chin, frantically typing down the information from her telephone contact straight into her computer.

At twenty-six, Jackie Spencer was desperate to move on to the big world of the national newspapers and felt she was merely marking time on The Inquirer. Not that there was anything wrong with working there. There was a great sense of camaraderie, the work was interesting and it meant something to her that it was a black newspaper. But the nationals were where the fame, glory and dollars lay and Jackie Spencer was the most ambitious journalist at The Inquirer.

'Reasonably good looking' was how she described herself and she made the most of what she had. Her tight-fitting power dress suits and immaculate bobbed haircut made her stand out in an office of more soberly dressed journalists. Her flirtatious nature and Welsh accent added to her charm. Born and brought up in Cardiff she had moved to London to go to University. After graduating she spent a year on a trade magazine before joining The Inquirer.

Jackie finished her telephone call and proceeded to open the day's post. She looked across to her colleague and sparring partner, Janice Pascal and smiled.

"Oh Janice luvee, this boyo from the House of Commons phoned this morning for you. Didn't catch his name, something Major or the other. There's a luvlee."

As a Taff in a city of cockneys, Jackie had long learned that the best way of avoiding having the piss taken out of her accent was to send it up herself by speaking in an exaggerated Welsh dialect. Janice shook her head and laughed.

"Oh Janice, wait. This one sounds like a potential date for you." Jackie was holding a ruled sheet of A4 paper in her hand while her eyes busily scanned the page.

"Wait Janice, listen to this:"

"Dear Miss Spencer,
I write to thank you for all the excellent articles you have written in The Inquirer. In particular your in-depth, factual and creative coverage of the Verone Baker case was both moving and thought provoking."

"Yeah 'creative' — that's the right word for your reporting," Janice cut in. Ignoring her, Jackie carried on reading.

"I don't need to tell you that there are some serious injustices going down in this country everyday. The courts and prisons of this country are full of young black men who in a just society have no place there. Justice is the construction of those who have the power to oppress and subjugate those in a weaker position. The laws are there for people with power, for their own self interest. How is it that a 57-year-old black woman can be murdered by the police, yet her killer walks free? Where is the justice in that? The Bible says 'an eye for an eye, a tooth for a tooth'. That is justice. I hope that you understand what I'm saying and that you have in some way got an idea of where I'm coming from.
Ordinary people have for too long just sat back and accepted things as they are. Well enough is enough. This is one man who's as mad as hell and he ain't gonna take it no more. Every dog has his day. Now is the time to settle the score.

An angry man."

Janice continued with her typing.
"What do you reckon Janice, does it sound like a

possibility for a date?"

"A date with a psychiatrist is what he needs. The man mad fe real," she said in an exaggerated patois. "You go deal wid 'im, Jackie. Let me know how you get on."

They joked about the letter some more then got on with the day's work. As a general news reporter the types of stories Jackie was expected to cover were wide and varied. However, she tried to avoid what she saw as the 'small interest' stories, the run-of-the-mill stuff like the opening of community centres, people trying to get re-housed by their council, or 'council to build new library' stories. With her focus so much on "getting into the mainstream" she was only really interested in doing those stories that would get her name noticed by the news editors on the nationals, or minor scoops that she would be able to rewrite, after they had appeared in The Inquirer, and sell to a national. In her co ntract it was forbidden for her to do any freelance for another publication, but her determination to move on had made her take the risk. On more than one occasion she had been summoned to the editor's office to explain how certain stories she'd been working on had appeared first in the nationals. She had denied all knowledge of them and as the stories were not accredited to a named journalist, the Editor had been forced to accept her word for the time being.

She was by nature not a cynical or ruthless person — typical characteristics of many journalists, but had lately adopted those traits believing them to be a pre-requisite for a £40,000 a year on The Sunday Times...

Lloyd ripped a small square of card from inside the Benson & Hedges packet and rolled it between his fingers into a cylindrical shape. He pushed it into the end of the spliff with a biro point and compressed the tobacco and ganja as he did so. After tucking the end of the rizla paper into the end of the card, he put it to his mouth and reached in his pocket for the lighter.

It was another hot, bright, summer's afternoon and sitting in the car with the warm breeze blowing through the wound-down window was making him feel sleepy. He didn't have time for sleeping, he had runnings to sort out. He turned up the radio, which as ever was tuned to Ruffneck FM, and smiled at the irony of the song's lyrics:

"M16 is an eradication gun,
Forty-Four is a Clint Eastwood gun,
Forty-Five is a bad bwoy gun, also a cowboy gun,
Twenty-Two is a lickle gun,
Winchester an indian gun..."

The spliff mellowed him out and he allowed it to gently chill him and lift him until he felt almost too sweet. He was in the car park outside his flat. He hoped Patrick would show soon. He had sat watching Patrick's black Audi for over two hours and knew that he would probably show soon. A glance at the car clock told him it was 2:15.

Lloyd was nervous. He knew Patrick more on a hail 'n' touch fist basis than as a close spar and he didn't know how break it to him. He didn't have time to think it over however, before Patrick came strutting across the yard, his long locks gently bobbing as he walked. Dressed in silver-grey, silk trousers, black Italian loafers and a criss baggy, white shirt, he was clearly going somewhere special. Lloyd stuck his head out of the car window.

"Yes, Lion. So you get married?"

Patrick turned and spotted the blue Sierra. Lloyd got out.

"Wha'ppen Lloydie? Wait, is summer holiday? Yuh nuh wuk today?"

53

They touched fists.

"I was just 'aving a lickle puss nap," Lloyd told the dread.

"More like a res' from pussy, innit?" Patrick said laughing.

Lloyd feigned a look of mock indignation and waved his hand at the dread, as if shooing away a child.

"Move yuhself, Jah P. Yuh know seh me nuh have time fe dem t'ings."

Both men laughed. Lloyd quickly cut the skylarking short.

"Listen Patrick, no offense intended by what I'm going to ask you, but I know you're a man who knows 'nuff people, seen. I need a 'matic and some bullets."

If he was surprised at the question or offended that the taxi driver would presume he knew gun dealers, it didn't show in Patrick's face. He rubbed his beard and looked upwards while he thought.

"Hol' on a second now. More time 'nuff ah me idren carry 'matic fe the i-tection, seen? But is mostly the white boys dem who deal with the hardware. Seen? But ah nuh nut'n, ah simple sump'n still. Jus' hol' on a second now."

The dread walked a few paces away and reached into his pocket. He took out a very small mobile phone and dialled a number. Lloyd couldn't make out what was being said but assumed that Patrick was dealing with his request. The dread finished his conversation and walked back to the Sierra.

"Yeah. I was speaking to my personal bredrin. Me tell him fe go sort out a lickle t'ing an' call back, seen? So hol' tight, jahman."

The two talked for another ten minutes about matters relating to cars without mentioning the gun. As a mechanic, cars were Patrick's great passion and he had worked on the vehicles of enough bad bwoys to know when it was prudent not to ask questions.

54

The discussion on the merits of an Audi five cylinder engine as opposed to a BMW straight six, were cut short by the beep of Patrick's mobile phone. Once again he walked several paces away from Lloyd to keep his conversation discreet. He returned after a brief time.

"Yeah Lloyd, t'ing sorted. 'Member boss, this is nothing to do with I. Yuh understan'?" He continued. "Yuh 'ave pen? Tek down the details."

The taxi driver took some paper and a biro from his car.

"At eight o'clock sharp, this evening yuh mus' reach to a pub on Old Kent Road name The Duke of Warwick. A white bwoy ah go check yuh there. Him seh fe wear a black baseball hat an' white T shirt so him can know you. Ah five hundred dollar him want fe the gun — cash. Yuh have dat?"

Lloyd nodded his head, thinking.

"Well star, me gone! Runnings haffe run. I gwan check yuh later, seen?" Patrick explained he was on a shopping mission for his woman and needed to make some moves. Lloyd thanked him and decided on giving the matter some more thought. He had about £260 in cash from fares in his flat. And he had a few hundred in the building society. He made tracks back inside Michael Connoly Gardens. He would have time to finish the letter he was writing to Jackie Spencer. He thought that yesterday's letter had not been clear enough and he should write again...

From the tone of his voice on the phone, it was clear that Ainsley Stewart was not pleased with the situation.

"Okay Jackie. It's not a problem... Look, I said it was okay. If you have to work late, you have to work late... I was just hoping that, for a change, we could have a quiet meal in, that's all... Yeah... I'll speak to you later... Bye."

Jackie Spencer let out a loud, deep sigh and dropped the phone back on the desk. She gripped her hair and pretended to pull it out as a sign of frustration.

"Ahhhhh men! Janice, you're looking for a man... I've got just the one for you. Name's Ainsley Stewart, 30-years-old, of Caribbean extraction, Oxford graduate, works as a public relations executive, good salary, company car and prospects, ambitious, handsome, extremely well-mannered and wants kids, but is also a pain in the backside, self-centred and likes to moan."

Janice looked up from the computer screen.

"The 'pain in the backside' sounds interesting. Have you told him to see a doctor?"

Janice's dry sense of humour was well known in the office. A year younger than Jackie, she had joined the newspaper as a 17-year-old typist and had worked her way up into the newsroom as a reporter. She was proud of her working-class origins and had no desire to join the buppiefied world of many of her university educated, reporter colleagues. Her down to earth, direct approach intimidated many of the men in the office who called her "unsophisticated" and "aggressive", but never to her face. She didn't suffer fools gladly in her work and everyone had to concede that when it came to getting the story, her no foolishness approach always delivered the goods. A well built woman around five feet-four tall, she had recently taken to wearing loose-fitting long dresses after an unfortunate occasion when a drunken Tory MP grabbed her shapely bottom at a small cheese and wine party at the Commons. She was wearing a tight-fitting mini skirt at the time and the sight of it have proved too much for the MP. Afterwards she punched him and threw him sprawling against a bookcase, warning him loudly and explicitly that: "If yuh touch me batty again, me gwan chop off yuh han'." The stunned MP made a beeline out of the reception.

Janice had taken an instant liking to "The Welsh Smallie" due to her unpretentious ways and the two quickly became tight spars.

"Listen Miss Spencer, I'm not looking for no man. Most of them cyaan deal with a strong woman like me. They just want some dibbi dibbi meek gal." She said it with a smile but Jackie felt that behind the joke the truth might not have been hiding too far away.

"So Jackie, is Ainsley giving you grief then?"

Jackie rested her chin on her hand and sighed.

"Yeah he didn't like it that I was going to have to stay late and catch up on some work. But it's alright when he has to do the same. Having a relationship and living with the person is pure stress, especially in a job like this."

Despite the road works the traffic was not as bad as Lloyd was expecting along the Old Kent Road. He had asked for directions twice to the Duke of Warwick and had cruised along the Road a few times, but he still couldn't find it. Just as he was about to pull over and ask the old man at the bus stop, he noticed it on the right hand side of the road. He turned into a side road on the left and parked the Sierra at the front of some flats.

The Duke of Warwick, with its mock-Tudor, white and timber framed front, was unknown territory for Lloyd. He had never had cause to go to any of the pubs in the area and was uncertain whether the natives would be friendly. As he walked in the door he felt several pairs of eyes move to him. He wasn't sure if it was because they knew he wasn't a local or because his face didn't fit.

Apart from an old black man sitting with a similar aged white woman by the fruit machine, his was the only black face in the pub. His baseball hat with an embroided 'X' in the middle, probably didn't help him to blend in. Mostly in their thirties and early forties, the drinkers in the pub were of traditional, white, working-class stock. He walked towards the bar returning the stares of some of the drinkers who averted his challenging gaze and continued drinking with their companions. The man behind the bar, arms folded, was leaning against the till watching Lloyd approach. He waited a few moments then sauntered across to the young black man.

"Yes, mate?"

It seemed less of an enquiry as to what drink he required, and more of a challenge. Lloyd decided to play it cool.

"Pint of lager... please."

The barman pulled the pint reluctantly and gave him the change. The taxi driver looked around and decided on occupying a table near the door. When the three men at the far side of the bar starting sniggering to the Bing Crosby song, Lloyd was in no doubt that this was not a pub that welcomed black customers.

"I'm dreaming of a white Christmas just like the ones I used to know," went the juke box. The men sniggered some more.

Lloyd watched the guy in the blue polo shirt and jeans coming towards his table and was already working out his strategy if needed. He would take him out with the large glass ashtray on the table and lose his pint glass in the face of the fat guy standing by the exit, followed by a rapid escape through the door. He had chosen this table carefully in the event of any trouble.

Of medium build and height the man looked in his early thirties. He had short brown hair and an expressionless face — which indicated he knew how to take care of himself. He put a cigarette in his mouth and carried on walking towards Lloyd's table.

"Excuse me mate, you got a light?"

Lloyd handed him his zippo. The man lit his cigarette and returned the lighter.

"You come from up East?" Lloyd nodded. "I think I've something you might be interested in. Leave it a minute san, then meet me outside."

Lloyd finished his pint and left.

Outside the pub, the man was surveying the area.

"You got the wonga, san?"

"Five hundred notes, right?"

"Yeah and it's a fuckin' bargain price for what I've got for ya. Let's go for a walk, yeah?"

They walked for about five minutes up the Old Kent Road then crossed over and went down a small no through road with bollards at the end, which led to the back of some run-down council flats.

The man stopped near the entrance to the communal rubbish room.

"Right, let's see the colour of your money. No offense."

The taxi driver didn't find the joke funny and gave the man a vicious stare.

"Listen bwoy," he said, emphasising the word 'bwoy', "you show me what you 'ave and then we sort out the finances."

The man was not happy with the arrangement and refused to deal until he was holding the money. The taxi driver had few options open to him and after arguing for a few minutes, decided he had to take a chance that it was not a skank. He had a blade strapped to his ankle and had already decided in the event of a set up, this feisty bwoy would be the first to get cut.

The man counted the money and tucked it into his trouser pocket. He directed the taxi driver inside the rubbish room and fetched a black bin bag from underneath a large dustbin on wheels.

It was starting to get dark and the lack of light in the stench-filled room made for an unpleasant sales office. The man took out a large automatic pistol. Its worn finish indicated that it had been well used during its lifetime.

Even though the deal had already been decided, the man couldn't resist going into his sales mode.

"This san, is ya genuine Colt forty-five automatic pistol. The real item, none of ya cheap Spanish copy. A real fuckin' man stopper this one. Makes a nine mill look like a fuckin' peashooter." He pulled out the magazine with his left hand. "Holds seven cartridges and one up the spout. A real fuckin' John Wayne gun this. Fuckin' blow a hole the size of a fist in some cunt's chest." He inserted the magazine in the handle of the pistol and pulled the slide backwards and forwards by way of a demonstration that it was functioning.

"This particular gun is totally clean, ain't been used in no robbery or nuffink like that. I've got a spare magazine and fifty rounds of useable ammo included in the price, which is a fuckin' pukka bargain. It's just that I need the wonga bad. It's a fuckin' steal mate."

The stench in the bin room was becoming unbearable and the taxi driver was glad to get outside. He pulled the baggy T shirt out of his jeans and pushed the gun into his waist band. He put the spare magazine into his back pocket and filled his pockets with the bullets which had been loose in the black bin bag. By this time the gun dealer had already disappeared through the flats. With the enveloping dusk and his loose T shirt concealing the piece he felt safe as he walked back to the car...

As she turned the key and opened the front door she could almost feel the bad vibes coming from inside.

"Jackie, I thought you said nine o'clock, man?"

"I'm really sorry Ainsley, I had to get that work done."

Jackie Spencer took off her jacket and draped it over the arm of a black leather armchair. Ainsley turned from watching the TV and picked up her jacket to put it on a hanger.

60

They had met just over 18 months ago and after a year she had moved into his designer-style Shepherd's Bush flat. The matt black bachelor furniture was a visible clue that this was still very much Ainsley's flat.

She made herself a coffee and joined Ainsley in the lounge. He remained silent, watching the television. Jackie was the first to break the silence.

"Have you eaten?"

"I cooked, expecting you at nine o'clock like you said. It got ruined so I flung it in the bin."

She held her coffee mug in both hands and sipped slowly in the armchair.

"Okay. Fine."

"No Jackie, it's not fine. I can't understand why, if you say you're going to be here at nine o'clock, you can't have the consideration to make sure you get here on time, or at least phone and let me know different."

Ainsley was clearly vexed and she thought it wise to retire from the potential field of battle.

"Ainsley, I'm really sorry. You're right, I should have phoned... I think I'll go and run a bath..."

The oil-stained remnants of the torn-up shirt lay on the right hand side of the table next to a small can of lubricating oil. The ammunition had been cleaned and polished, and was neatly arranged in five rows of ten shells a line. The brass cases and copper-coloured bullet heads gleamed in the focused light of the table's lamp. He carefully connected the slide of the pistol back onto the handle and pushed in the retaining pin.

He studied the diagram on the ripped book page again before pulling the slide back and cocking the hammer. With his arm outstretched he aimed at an imaginary target and squeezed gently on the trigger. The loud metallic click as the hammer struck home brought a satisfied smile to his face. It all seemed to be in perfect working order.

On his way back from the building society, where he withdrew most of the money in his account, he had stopped off at Hackney Central Library where he discreetly checked out various books on the mechanics of pistols, ripping out the relevant pages. By fortunate coincidence he had taxed a page illustrated with a construction diagram of a Colt .45 and this was now proving invaluable. Following the diagram, he had spent an hour grasping the construction of the weapon and had stripped down, cleaned and lubricated the main components using the cloth from his ripped shirt.

He was now ready to go to work on the ammunition. With the concentration of a surgeon he picked up the first case and tightly wrapped a piece of protective cloth around it. Carefully, he gripped the shell with some pliers in his left hand, while the small hack saw in the other cut through the copper casing and lead centre of the the bullet head. The job was finished by two crossed cuts of the saw on the top of the bullet.

The technique was a well known practice among gangsters to turn ordinary bullets into 'dum-dum' bullets. Unlike conventional bullets which left a neat 'clean' wound in human flesh, 'dum-dums' expanded on contact causing a large and slashed wound which increased the likelihood of death. The taxi driver had remembered a documentary where the method had been demonstrated and he was now putting his knowledge to use.

He completed eighteen of the bullets before he could feel a blister starting on his right hand. 'That will be enough for today', he thought to himself as he loaded the gun's magazine with the ammunition. The spare clip was similarly made, ready as a back up.

He wiped the excess oil off the weapon, and tucked it into his waist. It felt heavy and bulky. In the bedroom he admired his profile in the full length mirror then turned to address his reflection.

"You looking at me motherfucker?" he hissed, slowly, and menacingly. "Yeah you motherfucker!" He turned to face the mirror head-on and drew the gun rapidly from his waist, aiming at his reflection. Once more he turned to his side and challenged the imaginary enemy in the mirror. This time he tried it with his arms folded.

"Bwoy! You wan' sump'n...? Bwoy! Is who the fuck you lookin' at...? Who de raas you fuckin' staring at?"

He faced his challenger and pulled the gun more rapidly from his jeans waist band, then tried different variations on the same theme.

"Okay, come an' fuckin' deal with me then!" he barked his hands loose and ready at his side.

He pointed his right forefinger at his assailant, challenging him. "Yuh wan' tes'? Come tes' me, nuh."

Each time he drew his gun with even greater speed as he became familiar with its weight and balance.

He looked at his watch and it was nearly midnight. After leaving the gun and spare magazine under the mattress, he hid the remaining bullets in a box under the kitchen sink cupboard.

The night air was not as warm as he had expected, so he slipped on his leather jacket and half closed the zip. He had enough petrol to take him to Stockwell and back. It was now totally clear in his mind what he had to do. Now was the time to start putting his plan into operation. He lit the spliff he had made earlier on and put the car into gear.

FIVE

D amn. What you got in this case mate?" Lloyd struggled to lift the heavy battered suitcase into the boot of the Sierra.

"Oh, it's got weights for dumbbells in it." The man could see the taxi driver's puzzled look and further clarified the matter. "They ain't mine, they're me mate's... I'm just storing them for him."

From his anaemic-looking complexion and stick insect-like physique, Lloyd hadn't figured him to be the body building type. The explanation as to the weights' ownership satisfied his puzzlement. He helped the punky anarchist load his remaining bin bag luggage on to the back seat of the car and slammed shut the boot.

The army surplus clad punk noticed Lloyd's eyes scanning the row of dilapidated, multi-coloured terraced houses.

"They're chucking everybody out of 'em. Buildin' a fuckin' motorway through here. It's a fuckin' piss-take," he said in a broad cockney accent.

Claremont Road in Leyton was to disappear to make way for the M11 motorway, explained the teenage punk. Presently squatted by various artists and new-age travellers, the crumbling houses had once been the homes for many local families. Now the houses were to be pulled down and the Department of Transport was serving eviction notices. The punk was moving into a friend's flat on the Clapton Park Estate in nearby Hackney and this had been his second delivery trip of the day. Lloyd sympathised with the punk's plight.

"The system don't give a fuck for no one," the taxi driver added. "Not a fuck. But believe me, that can't gwan forever. Everything comes full circle and the chickens eventually come home to roost."

The punk wasn't convinced.

"The state is the tool of the rich and if you ain't got money you're treated as scum in this society."

"I'm hearing what you're saying mate and it's partly true, but sometimes..." He paused and broke into a strong Jamaican accent. "Dawg ah go bite the master's hand. Ya dig?"

The punk gave the matter some thought and nodded.

"Yeah... I hope that's true. My name's Terry."

"Respeck Terry, the name's Lloyd." The taxi driver gripped the steering wheel with his left hand and offered his right fist to the youngster who smiled and self-consciously touched fists with the man. Lloyd laughed at the punk's awkwardness. "Nuh worry yuhself, man, you'll soon get used to it. The speed at which black culture goes mainstream nowadays, you'll see John Major touch fists with the Queen soon."

The pair reasoned some more about the way things were, all the way to the council estate where the taxi driver helped Terry carry his things into the flat.

"Lloyd, ya want a beer, mate?"

Carrying heavy bags was thirsty work and the taxi driver was grateful for the offer of refreshment.

The two sat drinking in the front room.

"Terry, you smoke herb?"

The punk smiled and caught the bag of weed tossed to him. A packet of rizlas followed.

Terry put the opened bag to his nose and sniffed the prime Jamaican sensi.

"Cor, that smells like the business. We don't see much grass 'round 'ere. This is good shit, man. Where d'ya get this stuff from?"

Lloyd smiled, pleased that the youngster was impressed with the herb.

"Yeah, you white boys love smoking hash too much. Me personally, I stopped smoking the devil's herb when I was oh...fourteen or fifteen." Putting on an exaggerated cockney accent, he added. "Terry my san, you can't beat a good draw of Jam Down sensi, no way."

Terry revealed that he had recently served a term in the Scrubs for theft.

"I'm telling you mate, there were so many blacks in there," he recalled, "hardly any Asians, but loads of black guys. Some of them had been inside since they were fifteen and when you found out why, it was for some bollocks that a white guy wouldn't have been done for. That's how fucked up this shit is. I learned a lot in prison - best education there is. School of life, that's what I call it. It taught me that if you're gonna do crime, go for the big bucks like all those rich tossers in the city. So now I'm militant. I've got an appetite for destruction. I spend my time fuckin' things up for the system, you know what I mean...?

The taxi driver knew exactly what he meant. He wasn't so surprised that Terry questioned the wholesale incarceration of young black males in the country's prisons. There were some conscious white people now relating to this. Terry even suggested a black man's revolution to change things.

"Yeah a revolushan. Don't worry about the cops. What you need is an angry black man who needs cash money to take care of them. He'll be in no more danger than the average black man goes through every day."

They sat and smoked three more killer spliffs before Lloyd realised how much time was moving on. He had been taking liberties at Swift Cars and knew they wouldn't put up with his slackness for much longer. He had given too many excuses about why he was late, or away from the office for so long, or why he didn't reply on the radio. He knew the boss Sanjay owed him a favour, but there were limits to how far he could stretch things.

Terry's eyes were red and glazed. His head rested on the arm of the settee and his body lay sprawled along the length of the seat. His black army boots rested on the sofa's other arm. He was wasted. Lloyd finished off the last of his beer and stood to leave.

"Terry, does your mate want to sell those weights?"

The punk raised his head and blinked his eyes.

"Wot?"

"I was thinking of getting some weights. Does your mate want to flog his?"

"Yeah. He ain't bothered about 'em. I've got the bars and things in the other room... Gizza tenner an' they're yours."

The deal struck, Lloyd struggled to carry the weights back to the car while Terry brought down the bars and collars.

"Terry my san, nice to make your acquaintance. Me gaan!"

The punk made a fist.

"Respeck Lloyd. You fuckin' messed me up with that weed, I'm tellin' ya mate."

The taxi driver laughed at the youngster's new found blackness and touched fists a final time as he climbed in the Sierra.

"Cheers for the weights, Terry. Later."

It was 4:30 pm when he parked in the side road a few doors down from Swift Cars. He was relieved to see that Sanjay was at the controller's seat and not Millie. He was in no mood to take a tongue-lashing from the woman. Sanjay looked up from behind the glass screen and muttered a greeting. His mind seemed preoccupied with something.

Lloyd reached into his back pocket and took out a

packet of chewing gum. He opened one and offered another to Sanjay.

"Oh cheers. Damn paperwork. It's nothing but a bloody headache from these VAT people." He chewed the gum, while trying to make sense of the sheet of figures in front of him.

In his early thirties, the Asian's dream of owning a string of mini-cab firms by the time he was 35, seemed to be getting more remote by the day as he discovered that running one's own business was a full-time headache. His jet black hair had already revealed its first traces of grey and his forehead carried a permanent frown.

Sanjay rubbed the scar near his mouth with his right forefinger as he always did when he was stressed. Although his moustache partly concealed the knife wound, two inches of scar was still visible on his cheek; a grim souvenir of his childhood days on the mean, race-hate streets of Whitechapel. The scar made him self-conscious and he didn't like to look anyone in the eye when he talked.

"Hey, Mr Loverman, so this is where you keep your mistress!" It was the heavy West African voice of one of the Nigerian drivers, Tunde. Lloyd turned around to see who he was addressing.

"Stockwell, eh? They say the women down there are very easy." With a large grin on his face, Tunde examined a torn out page from an A to Z, which had an area in Stockwell circled in red felt pen. Lloyd felt his back pocket and realised it had fallen when he pulled the chewing gum out. He leant forward to retrieve the paper but Tunde pulled it away.

"Now let me see if I recognise any of the roads. I have a few women down there. Who knows, we could be doing the same girl." It was meant in jest and the two other drivers in the office saw the joke. It was however the wrong move. When the Nigerian looked up and saw

Lloyd's cold eyes and expressionless face, he realised it.

Lloyd reached forward and squeezed the sides of the man's round cheeks till his lips were squashed open like a fish's mouth. His hand held the man's jaw in a vice-like hold with Tunde too terrified to move. Lloyd held the grip as beads of sweat trickled down the dark, shiny skin of the Nigerian's forehead. Lloyd's face remained cold and without expression. There was a shocked silence in the office, no one dared to say anything or move.

"Don't tes' me. Gimme the map..." He released his grip and the frightened man handed over the map, which Lloyd then tucked into his back pocket. Then he lit a cigarette. The silence was broken by the ringing of the phone. Sanjay instructed the Nigerian to take the booking and a sense of near-normality was restored.

Hours later and Lloyd was still thinking about the incident with Tunde. True, the man was feisty and deserved a good slap, but he regretted bringing attention to the map and himself like that. Still, it was done, and that was it.

At that moment he thought of his mother sitting in the armchair consoling an 11-year-old Phillip Baker who was in tears after his brand new bicycle had been stolen from outside the local sweet shop.

"What is done and past help, is past grief" she said to his little brother, wisely. It was only years later, when he saw the expression in a book, that he realised that it was a line from Shakespeare and not a saying from Yard.

The crowds seemed to be walking in slow motion along Notting Hill Gate and the neon-lit shop fronts suddenly seemed strangely unfamiliar and like a film set. The rear lights of the slow-moving cars in front seemed hazy and slightly out of focus. He remembered he hadn't eaten all day and suddenly he felt hungry and thirsty. He turned left down a side road and parked up.

The hamburger and fries tasted better than they were

and the coffee was much needed. The glitzy fast food restaurant was a sea of constantly changing faces and the many different voices merged together into one droning noise reverberating inside his head. Maybe it was too many beers and spliffs on an empty stomach? He felt like he was invisible, travelling in limbo, observing every little gesture of all these aimless people. The noise became too much; he needed a walk.

Outside, people passed him by in a kind of slow motion too, moving with no purpose. Why were they walking down this street at this time? His head felt hot.

He walked into a a supermarket and bought a large bottle of water. He noticed that everyone on the street was staring at him, but he couldn't do anything about it. He poured the water over his head and it formed into a small puddle on the pavement. His head felt much better: Cooler and clearer. Time to carry on working.

The breeze blowing through the car's window was helping get things in focus, clearing his mind. The drive down Oxford Street was fine and by the time he got to the junction with Regent Street everything seemed to be back in perspective. He turned left up Portland Place and passed the BBC on his right, straight up, through both sets of traffic lights and turned right at the crescent. He waited at the traffic lights at the junction with the Marylebone Road. It was 11:15pm and the roads were surprisingly light with traffic.

The lights changed to green and the Sierra pulled away. Regent's Park Road was empty of traffic and, as ever, dimly lit. As he glanced in his rear view mirror he could see the single headlight and blue flashing light turn off from the Marylebone Road and approach rapidly behind him. It wasn't a pull but obviously a radic answering an emergency call. He looked at his speedo; it read 40 mph. He glanced back at the light coming up quickly behind him. He could work out that it was a police motorcyclist and he could see no other vehicles behind the biker. There were no cars coming down the opposite side of the road either.

He could hear the roar of the BMW bike's engine getting closer. He indicated left and started to pull in to the curb. In his right hand door mirror he could see the bike about to pass him. As it got close he made his move. He slipped down a gear, depressed the accelerator pedal and the Sierra's two-litre engine caused the car to rapidly pick up speed. At the same time he violently heaved the steering wheel to the right.

Concentrating on the road as he was, the move took the motorcyclist totally by surprise. Lloyd felt a thud as the front wing of the Sierra hit the knee of the rider and sent the bike veering off to the right. A look of horror on his face, the cop frantically fought to control the machine but the front wheel was already sliding hopelessly, causing the bike to start falling on its side.

Lloyd heard the massive crash but he was too far up the road to see what had happened. He had changed into fourth and was now turning right, off Regent's Park Road towards Camden. He jumped two red lights and was soon crossing Camden High Street, taking the back roads towards Islington.

His heart was beating like the engine of a steam train and a huge rush of adrenaline had enveloped his body. He had never experienced such a high mix of fear and excitement before. He kept expecting to see a blue flashing light behind him but it never came and his excitement grew. He imagined that the front of his car was massively damaged and other drivers would look and know how this had happened. He feared that the police would be setting up road blocks all over town and the driver of every car would be stopped and their vehicle inspected. Suppose the cop was still alive and remembered the Sierra's registration number from his hospital bed? Suppose his dying words were the registration number?

Fuck them all! Fuck 'em! Police behaved like they had the authority to kill black mothers, so fuck 'em. If they were going to come for him tonight, then they had fucking better be ready for a fight. He wasn't going to come quietly. He would take a few of them out with him!

He passed through Hackney keeping his eyes on the rear-view mirror throughout and drove straight back to his yard. Inside, he took the Colt from under his bed and put the spare magazine into his jacket pocket. He built up a spliff to calm his nerves and lay on his bed with the 'matic resting on his chest. He drew hard on the good herb and blew a long white trail of white smoke from his lungs. After a few minutes his heartbeat slowed to a pace at which he could think more clearly.

As he lay there pulling on a spliff he thought about all the possible clues that could lead to his capture. At this stage, arrest was unthinkable; he still had too many other plans on the drawing board. Then he thought about the fare he dropped in Acton, could they provide the police with any information? No, he decided, there was nothing to link Acton with Regent's Park. But were there any witnesses? That was a possibility he could do nothing about, he concluded. Anyway, the car was not even registered in his name. He'd bought it six months ago with a year's tax and had not got round to sending off the registration documents. The person who he had bought it from didn't even know who he was or where he lived, so that was no problem. Thoughts went round and round in his mind — all the possible links — and he came to the conclusion that there were none likely to lead the cops to him.

He finished his spliff and headed back to Swift Cars. As he entered the office, Sanjay looked worried. Lloyd had been gone so long that he expected to get his marching orders, but Sanjay was concerned about something else.

"That fucking, racist bastard was here just thirty minutes ago. He wanted to know where you were."

"Who you talking about, man?"

"You know that fucking fat bastard who came in the other morning drunk. The one with the tattoos."

Lloyd remembered the beating he gave to 'Cockney Wanker' in Woodford.

"Listen Lloyd, he had a knife. He said he was going to cut you up. He was serious and definitely looking for a fight. Maybe I should call the police?"

"No bother wid dat," the taxi driver said calmly. "Mek him come."

"Okay, it's your throat... There's a pick-up on Roman Road to Stratford. I told them a car would be there ten minutes ago."

As he left the cab office and walked to the side street where his car was parked, Lloyd noticed the silhouette by his motor. He ducked against the front of the corner shop and crouched down low. Slowly, he popped his head round the wall and peered down the side road where he clearly saw the figure of a man dart into the alley right next to where the Sierra was parked. His car was in a dimly-lit, no-through road with no houses, only businesses. Yes, it was the perfect place for an ambush, he thought. He considered the options. He had to go after him and personally put a foot up his arse, but even with the 'matic it would be foolish to approach the car from this direction. The cockney could be holding a sawn-off in the cover of the dark alley, the taxi driver would be a sitting duck. Lloyd decided on the best strategy, then made his move.

He retraced his steps lithely back to the cab office and crossed over to the other side of the busy Bow Road, careful not to be spotted by his prey. He would wait for the right moment.

He waited ten minutes before his opportunity arrived. If he timed it right, the slow-moving articulated lorry travelling along the opposite side of the road would play its part. As it neared the side road Lloyd began sprinting as fast as he could to reach alongside the lorry. His timing was impeccable. The lorry had obscured perfectly any possible line of vision from the alley. He then crossed back over the road and walked down the next side road adjacent to where his car was parked. The alleyway linked the two roads, but as it curved, it was only possible to see the other entrance when one got near to the middle of the alley. Lloyd pulled the .45 from his waist, pulled the slide back, and clicked off the safety catch. Now he was ready to smoke the motherfucker.

Gingerly, he crept slowly along the alley. It was essential that he had the element of surprise and that meant moving slowly and quietly. For the second time that evening he could feel his heart beat so quickly that it hurt. Step by step he moved, hardly breathing, stopping only to calm his nerves. As he pressed himself against the wall of the alley and walked stealthily forward he came closer and closer to the centre. Eventually he had the man in his sight. His back was against the alley wall near the entrance, his head turned to the side, looking out towards the car and the side road. In his right hand was a vicious-looking machete.

Once again Lloyd paused to consider his options. He knew he was up against a dangerous man, but considered himself just as dangerous, if not more so. Should he just bumrush the cunt now? No, there was still a good chance that the prey might escape or have time to pull a shooter from his jacket. He dismissed that idea and decided that the only sensible approach was to keep his nerve and proceed with stealth.

Inch by inch he moved like a snake down the alley, at

each step praying that 'Cockney Wanker' would not decide at that moment to take a piss or have a smoke. His heart beat even faster. He had never fired a gun before and knew that unless he got in at point blank range, the chances of hitting his target were slim. Point blank range also meant getting within slashing zone of the cockney's machete. He had to make sure there were no mistakes but there was no way for him to avoid the fact, he reasoned, that he was frightened to death. He could still end up with a cut throat if he wasn't careful. He continued creeping forward, very slowly, trying to keep his blood pressure low.

He was now so close that with another step he could touch the shoulder of the fat man with his arm outstretched, and he was so quiet he could hear his lungs ventilating. He was nearly there, just a little bit more, a little bit more...

Whether it was sixth sense or the sound of his clothes rustling, Lloyd didn't know. 'Cockney Wanker' suddenly turned his head. It was too late; the hunter had got his prey.

"Suck on that!" were the last words the cockney was to hear in this life. As the taxi driver spoke he pushed the gun hard into the belly of the fat man and pulled the trigger.

The boom of the big automatic was muffled by the flesh of the cockney's gut, but in the restricted confines of the alley it sounded like a major explosion. The big man was lifted an inch off his feet by the impact and slammed hard against the alley wall. He staggered for a moment with a puzzled look on his face. The machete fell to the ground. Then his legs folded underneath him and he slid down the wall. He ended up in a seating position with his back to the wall. His eyes were open and there was a sickening gurgling sound coming from his open mouth.

'Shit, he's still alive. Fuck. What to do?' Lloyd

75

panicked. He wanted to use the gun again, but was worried the noise would attract the attention of the police at the nearby Bow Road nick or anyone else in the vicinity. He looked around for suitable weapons. The dying man's machete would be too messy. There was nothing else. Lloyd tucked the Colt into his waist and went to open the Sierra's boot. He returned with a jump start lead and tied it round the white man's neck. Grabbing hold of both ends he pulled as hard as he could until he was sure there was no life left in the man's body. Then, lifting him under his shoulders, he dragged the cockney to the back of the car. He was only just able to lift the heavy body into the boot and his back hurt. He picked up the machete and threw it into the boot. By a stroke of luck he stepped on the ejected bullet case and was able to retrieve it. With the aid of a bottle of water from the boot and an oily rag, he cleaned the blood from his hand and did his best to wash away some of the blood in the alley. Some soil, stomped around the path, also helped in the concealment...

When he arrived at Roman Road, the long-haired guy with the guitar case was not very happy at waiting three quarters of an hour for a cab.

"Bloody hell mate I thought you weren't coming. Shall I stick this case in your boot?"

The man was already at the rear of the Sierra with his hand on the catch. Lloyd caught the man's wrist —just in time —and held it firmly.

"Nah mate, nah. Full of junk, boss. Stick it on the back seat."

The taxi driver puffed out a sigh of relief as the man deposited his instrument in the rear seat.

On his return From Stratford the Lloyd thought hard about what to do with the body in the boot. There was nowhere that seemed the right place. He resolved to sort it out some time tomorrow.

The musician was his last fare for the night and he drove off the motorway. As he took his usual turning off the Bow Road and eventually turned into Michael Connoly Gardens, he noticed the blue flashing light of a police car in the car park.

SIX

D ear Jackie...... my mission seems to have become steadily clearer. As the man says 'talk is cheap', and I agree. There are too many who spout rhetoric about what is wrong in this society but then do nothing to change anything. I used to be like that. I felt powerless to correct things that were wrong but now I can see it all so clearly. The ghetto is like a survival test. As I said in my previous letters, there ain't no justice in this country. There ain't no justice — just me!

You are now about to witness the strength of street justice. I have started down my chosen path and there is now no going back. I may be just one man against the system but I'm determined not to go quietly. See I've got this problem, a big problem, cops don't like me so I don't like cops. They wanna test me, so believe me Jackie, those bastards will pay and pay hard. I am determined to give it 100%. To the max.

It's time to retaliate on the fucking police. Last night was only the start. I read in the paper that the motorcycle cop had died and I am glad to hear that. He was the first of many. By the time they finally catch up with me there's going to be a bloodbath of dying cops. The more I eliminate, the more respect they'll learn.

When I first wrote to you I wanted someone who could grasp what was going on in my head. I was uncertain and confused. Now it is all clear as day. I know what must be done and I write not to ask for your understanding, but for you to one day chronicle my mission and my possible last days in this life. I will be writing to you again. Keep the faith.

Once just an angry man. Now an angry man with a mission!

The Cop Killer.

Ainsley Stewart shook his head and passed the letter back to his woman.

"Man, that geezer is seriously out to lunch... You say this is the third letter he's sent?"

Jackie looked briefly at the letter again before folding it back into the envelope.

"Yeah, the third one. You know there was a small story in yesterday's Evening Standard about that policeman who collided with a lamp post near Regent's Park, but the story said that it was a tragic accident."

Ainsley poured her another cup of filter coffee and removed her used plate. He shouted from the small kitchen which adjoined the lounge.

"I can't believe you haven't called the police. The streets are full of nutters. What are you going to do if he starts stalking you, eh? That's how it starts, you know. First the letter, then 'pap', 'pap', 'pap' with a gun. I would call the police as soon as possible, and I mean that."

"Ainsley, there's always some mad person writing to The Inquirer. Sometimes they even turn up at the reception... you just have to humour them. They're harmless."

He popped his head round the kitchen doorway.

"Listen Jackie," he said in mock patois with a smile, "any fool-fool come trouble you, tell dem they better not ramp wid yuh, 'cause they're also ramping wid me. You understan'?"

"Oh Ainsley you're such a hard man." She licked her lips and purred in an exaggeratedly sexy voice. "And so irresistible when you put on your Shabba voice. Why don't you come here and show me how hard you really are!"

Ainsley smiled at her expectantly...

Lloyd turned the volume control up some more and

carried on cutting up the newspaper. A vintage roots record, a hit from the days of way back, boomed out of the hi-fi's resonating speakers.

"Do you remember the days of slavery?

Do you remember the days of slavery?" asked the wailing lyrics.

His task with the scissors finished, he pinned the newspaper cutting to the notice board. 'POLICE MOTORCYCLIST DIES IN ROAD SMASH'. The cop killer read the last paragraph again, smiling to himself: "no other vehicle was believed to have been involved in the death of the officer." It had gone like a dream.

He smiled and took a drink from his Tennants can. He polished off the remnants of his Chinese take-away and dropped the foil containers into the kitchen dustbin. The Orchid Garden could always be relied upon to do a nice chow-mein, he reflected.

Making himself comfortable on the sofa, he read again the letter that came that morning from Phillip in Jamaica. His three week stay had turned into a nine week one but he said he would be back any day now, as his university term started in October. While the summer in Britain had been good, and for September it was still very warm, he envied his brother's long escape to the sandy shores, blue seas and unlimited sunshine of their ancestral homeland. Lloyd wondered how his brother was getting on with his girlfriend, Sharron, and whether if he would move in with her on a permanent basis. Since his mother's shooting just over a year ago, Phillip rarely stayed at the family home in Navarino Street, preferring to spend most of his time at Sharron's place.

Lloyd thought about the money that could be coming to him from the police damages settlement and the sale of his mother's house. If he hadn't embarked on his mission, it would have been something to look forward to. He could have stopped working and moved out to a little house in the countryside as he had always envisaged, and taken time out to write a book. He had a wicked black love story in his head which he was sure those boys at the X Press would want to publish. The money would be of little use to him now however, but it was important that he made a will so it would all pass to Phillip without a hitch. He made a mental note to visit a solicitor in the next few days and sort the matter out.

It could all end at any moment. It was a dangerous course he was on, he pondered. 'Fuck, it came so close to the end the other night', he reasoned. He had returned to his flat with a loaded gun in his waist, a dead cockney in his car boot, and blood stains on his clothes and shoes. He had arrived at the time as the police car that was carrying the two radics. Fortunately they were more concerned about taking a drunken wife beater down to the station. Otherwise it could have all been over. The cop killer took a deep breath as he contemplated how nearly the night had ended badly.

Putting the letter back on the table, he took up one of his new purchases and skimmed through the pages. That afternoon he'd stopped on the Caledonian Road to get some parts for the Sierra and he had noticed a secondhand bookshop. He had gone in out of curiosity and had found U.S.-published books in there. 'Black Medicine' was a guide to the most effective ways to kill a man using bare hands, knife, club or garrote. 'Improvised Munitions and Explosives' said the blurb on the back of the paperback book, was a comprehensive guide to making explosives and weapons using easily obtained chemicals and other household materials. Written in pseudo-military speak, the books masqueraded as military training manuals, but their likely uses probably had nothing to do with winning any conventional war.

For the cop killer, finding these books took on a special, almost spiritual, significance. It was more than a coincidence that he came across the bookshop and found these books on the shelves; it was meant to be, he reasoned.

One section of the book was titled: 'TAKING OUT A SENTRY'. *The most effective means of attack is by approach from the rear of the person. This is important for the element of surprise, for offering less physical resistance and for access to vulnerable areas of the body. Your left hand should cover the mouth of the the enemy, at the same time as the head is pushed up to expose the vulnerable front area of the neck. The hand on the mouth will muffle any noises or shouts from the target. With the knife in your right hand, use the centre of the blade to slash a two-inch gash across the windpipe and main neck artery. A fair degree of firm pressure will be required to sever the windpipe and it is most effective to move your hand in a top to bottom slashing movement to achieve this. Simply putting the knife to your opponent's throat and attempting to pull it into his throat will not be effective.'*

The cop killer turned page after page, studying the information and making mental notes as if he was examining a D.I.Y manual or a book on car mechanics. Lloyd liked to be prepared and he was determined that when he went into 'battle' he would be as ready like Rambo.

He checked his watch. 9:00 pm. There was time for an hour's worth of exercise. He fell to the ground and executed a hundred press-ups in rapid time, then turned over and began on the same number of sit-ups. When his stomach and arm muscles were tight, he started on some stretching exercises. With his bare feet resting on two flat bits of wood, he slowly slid downwards, legs apart until he could go no longer, then held it there until sweat dripped from his forehead, his face contorted with pain. After a breather, he skipped through some shadow boxing moves then turned to the weights he'd purchased from Terry the punk. They were seeming like a timely

82

acquisition. He had subjected himself to some punishing workouts; pushing weights was one of the fastest ways to tone your muscles. The day after the first session his muscles had been in agony, but he ignored the pain and continued pumping the metal. Now, after only his third session, his muscles had become accustomed to the brutal new regime. Varying between one routine to the next he worked his body like a man possessed. His vision was clear and the pain ceased to come into the equation of sensory perceptions. Sweat poured off his body and his heart pounded violently but he refused to be put off from his goal. The pumping reggae bass line of the ragga tape in the background helped him overcome the muscle ache and physical exhaustion. An hour later he broke off from his evening's training. He ran himself a bath and relaxed in the tub. A fresh spliff was his own personal reward for the workout. He lay with his feet resting on the taps, taking a soothing toke from the refreshing herb. As ever, his mind focused on trying to unravel some of the circumstances of his mother's death. Why had the police gone to the house in the first place? He knew that Phillip had nothing to do with drug dealing, so why would the police plant the coke? He went over the questions and the possible answers in his mind, as he had done countless times over the last twelve months. He thought also about the Inspector, in his comfortable Wanstead home, watching the television with his wife and kids at this very moment. What were the Inspector's feelings at that moment when he extinguished the life from his mother? How would the Inspector feel when his time came to die? He pulled out the plug and ended the question time session.

He tuned the radio into a pirate station and started to tidy things up in the lounge.

"Dis is the one an' only, one hundred per cent pure

*wickedness, Rrrrrrruffneck FM. Dem call we the Assassin
'cause we ah play pure killer tunes an' we nah tek no prisoners,
fe true. Hackney posse, hol' tight. Tottenham massive,
rrrrrespeck. Stokey rude bwoys, big up... An' to all the south
London pirates- yuh cyaan tes' we. Fe true!"*

The deep, broad Jamaican accent of the deejay
smoothly rode the riddim line of the raw dancehall re-mix
with all the experience of a true sound man.

It had been a long time since he'd been to a dance and
the cop killer thought about checking one out soon. He
was running out of time so he might as well enjoy his
winning run. He held a clutch of aces for the moment, but
he could be dealt a renk hand at the next cut of the pack.
He glanced at his watch. Time was getting on. He had
runnings to take care off. He picked up the nylon rope
he'd bought the day before and put it into a carrier bag.
His preparations were cut short.

'Bang, bang, bang!' He rushed to the bedroom and
grabbed the Colt.

'Bang, bang'. It was louder this time. He considered
not opening the door, but that wouldn't make any odds; if
it was the police they could easily hear the music and
would know that someone was in, he reasoned. With the
gun in his right hand behind his back, he opened the door
six inches with his left hand.

"Oh sorry to knock on your door so hard, but I didn't
know if you could hear me."

She looked about twenty-four, blonde-haired, pretty
with an apologetic smile. Her accent was posh southern
and she was clearly not a native.

"Hello I'm Miriam, I moved in today, next door," she
said, pointing to the open door of her flat. "Sorry to
trouble you. I don't know if you know anything about
electrics, but all the lights have gone off in my flat."

It was such a relief not to see a squad of radics in the

hallway that the cop killer smiled and let out a nervous laugh.

"Oh yeah, sure, no problem. Wait there, I'll get a torch." He shut the door and leant against it.

"Phew!" he muttered to himself.

Lloyd quickly located the problem of the lights to a contact breaker that simply needed resetting. Light returned to the flat before long.

"Thanks a lot. Can I get you a cuppa?"

"Yeah, okay. You smoke spliff? I've got some herb that will go down nicely with the coffee."

Miriam's face turned a deep red with embarrassment. Seconds later the head of a middle-aged woman popped around the open door of the lounge.

"Oh this is my mum... and these are Monty, Billy and Henry." The heads of three King Charles spaniels also appeared. Mother had a sweet grin on her face.

"Did I hear someone mention something about ganja? Yes please! Right on, rastaman!" Miriam turned and stared at her mother, her mouth open...

He threw the bag of rope over and looked again to ensure no one was about. With a short run and a leap he got his hands onto the top of the wall and slowly pulled himself up before jumping over the other side. He landed with a thud on the concrete yard. He turned and looked at the metal door which provided an access between the yard and the street on the other side of the wall. The large concrete block he had pushed against the door to keep it shut was still there. He walked across to the large broken-down storage shed and shone his torch inside; the dirty oil-stained tarpaulin was in the same place he had left it.

Once a successful manufacturer of high quality machine tools, the Matthew's factory had stood empty for a number of years, having fallen victim to cheaper technology from the Far East. The site, near Hackney Marshes, had gradually fallen into disrepair and was now all but derelict. A popular spot for fly-tippers and dumpers of domestic rubbish, the Matthew's factory now provided a dumping area for a very different kind of unwanted waste.

The body of the Cockney Wanker had been in the boot of the cop killer's Sierra for almost 24 hours whilst he deliberated about the best possible means of its disposal. Even after a thorough washing and the liberal application of various household air fresheners, the car still carried the faintly obnoxious odour of death in it. Under cover of darkness, he had deposited the body in the factory outbuilding, until he had the materials to make concealment of the body more effective.

As he pulled back the tarpaulin the black, bulging, lifeless eyes of his victim stared up at him. Death had bloated his body and the unusually warm September climate had already got to work on decomposing the grotesque, pallid-looking corpse. The smell was nauseous and Lloyd was desperate to get the job done.

With the lock knife from his pocket, he cut four, metre-long lengths of rope from the bundle in the bag. Securing a length to each ankle and wrist, he dragged the body as close as possible to the side of the disused canal which ran alongside the yard. The abandoned metal-reinforced concrete nearby were ideal for the task. He securely tied the other ends of the four pieces of rope to the large blocks of concrete. With a large piece of timber pushed under the back of the corpse, he levered the body into its watery resting place.

With a loud 'splosh' the concrete blocks sank to the bottom of the murky, weed-filled canal. After waiting a minute or so, Lloyd shone his torch into the canal. Apart from a few gentle ripples on the surface and a disturbed patch of green surface weed, nothing of the body could be seen. He walked to the metal door, which was normally open, and heaved the concrete obstruction out of the way. His head peered round the door while he made sure the coast was clear. The street running alongside the factory contained no houses, so his car was the only one parked there. To a passing police car it would have stuck out a mile. He paused only to load a large block of concrete and the bag of rope into the boot of his Sierra before he departed from the dimly-lit industrial area.

The car's clock read 1:30 am. There was still some unfinished business to take care of, but he first needed something to eat. He contemplated what the food options were and settled on some hot tuna bagles from the 24-hour bakery in Dalston's Ridley Road.

Although the road had been swept there was still evidence in the gutters of the daily fruit and veg market located in the street. As a popular late-night take-away for both local and not-so-local clubbers and rude bwoys, there was usually an assortment of some criss-looking vehicles parked outside. Tonight, a brace of blacked-out, low slung, BeeEm three-two-fives were parked indiscreetly outside the bakery. Three yard men were standing by a wicked-looking, gleaming, black Saab convertible. One of the men in green baggy trousers, matching silk shirt and heavy gold 'cargo' around his neck, had his arm around the waist of a large-bottomed, mampy-sized girl dressed in a short, tight, white dress and sequinned baseball boots. It was an everyday scene amongst Hackney's late-night ravers.

Situated on a corner site, the bright interior lights of the bakery lit up the outside street via its large front and side windows. As Lloyd stepped into the doorway, two ill-mannered youths coming out from the shop pushed their way past him, causing the cop killer's shoulder to knock hard against the shoulder of one of the ragga-styled youngsters. The young man muttered a curse and gave the cop killer an evil look. Lloyd turned and returned the stare. He wasn't looking for trouble but if this rough yout' wanted to make something of it, he would teach him some respect. The older man's cold, expressionless, penetrating 'if yuh bad' stare unnerved the youth, who decided it was not a good idea to test his manhood on this occasion. He carried on walking but held his stare with the cop killer for several paces. Lloyd watched the pair stroll further down the road and get into a customised purple Astra GTE convertible with a white hood.

The bakery was crowded with the usual cross-section of late-night London life. Trendy white dance funksters, rude bwoys, soul boys, batty bwoys, ragga gals, slack gals, the drunk, and insomniacs squeezed into the shop, all impatiently waiting to be served. The three women behind the counter rushed to get the orders in and out of the microwave ovens, as some of the rudest customers cursed them for taking too long with an order.

The cop killer waited in the queue and tried not to think about the pleasant small of warm bread that filled the air. He was hungry and impatient.

"Lloyd?"

The voice was familiar but he wasn't certain. The cop killer turned round. There was a slight pause as he took in her features. When he took in who is was he began wondering what she was doing so far north of the river, and what his reaction should be.

"Er, Sonia what you doing here? How are you? Long time, innit?" He felt awkward and it made the woman feel the same. He glanced at Sonia's male friend.

"Oh, this is Errol."

"Errol, this is Lloyd."

Errol and Lloyd looked self glanced at each other, nodded and said a muted 'hello'.

"So Lloyd, what you been doing with yourself? You

still cabbing?"

"Yeah, you know, but I'm checking out some business ideas at the moment," he lied.

It had been nearly a year and a half since he'd gone out with Sonia but he hadn't forgotten how she used to comment on his 'lack of ambition'. She looked good, as fit and attractive as he remembered her and that happy sparkle was still in her eyes. Five foot, four inches with curves in all the right places, Sonia carried herself with the kind of indefinable sexiness most men couldn't resist. That black dress looked like it was made to show off the best of her, thought Lloyd.

"That's good Lloyd. You're a clever guy, I always said that. You could make a lot more of yourself."

Even after eighteen months the tune was still the same and the lyrics hadn't changed. Lloyd struggled to think what to say next, but then Sonia quickly added:

"I'm really sorry about your mum. It's terrible. I wanted to go to her funeral but I didn't know if you'd want me there. You know what I mean?"

"That's alright. I got the flowers and card. Respeck to you for sending them. Appreciated."

They chatted for a few more awkward minutes before Lloyd wished her the best and headed for his car.

"Yeah, we've got a caller on the line now. Sandra from Islington, come in sis."

"Hello, Robbie, this discussion about 'should baby fathers take more responsibility for dem pickney?' Yeah, right, I think it's wrong to try and make out that all men don't care for their youts. I have two kids, and although I don't live with their father, yeah? The guy is like an angel to them and supports me to the max, with money and all that business. I say to the sisters, stop dissing the black man and saying, 'dem all de same'. 'Cause it nuh true... Respeck Robbie, I love yah show bad."

"Respeck to you Sandra. Remember people, support your woman, support your man... You're listening to the Smooth Operator, Robbie Mac, on Ruffneck FM, mashing up the airways. I'm going to drop a new tune on you that's fast becoming a big hit with the ladies. On X Press Records, here's Mr Patrick Augustus with a reworking of The Chi-Lites 'Have You Seen Her', now appropriately entitled 'Baby Father'. East London, hol' tight.

Lloyd ate his tuna bagels while the car's radio pumped the tune beamed from the Ruffneck FM control tower in Tottenham. His mind was on Sonia. Scenes from their two years together started playing on the big screen of his mind. He recalled Sonia's 23rd birthday at Night Moves club when she got so drunk she had to spend the whole of the next day ill in bed. And the time they drove down to Brighton on the spur of the moment and spent the day chilling out on the beach. He remembered also the blazing row one New Year's Eve, about where he was going in life.

Good times and bad times, they had shared both. He was sorry it had not worked out, but they were different people wanting different things out of life. Those days seemed light years away from the last year when he had fallen into a deep, dark hole that was impossible to escape from. He knew he had changed, but he couldn't quite remember who he used to be. The numbness had slowly changed to bitterness. In turn, that had become an anger that seemed to consume him. A part of his head still rationalised that the odds pointed to self destruction. But his soul no longer gave a fuck. Anger, revenge, justice and nihilism were the raw motivators now. The 'better life' he had once glimpsed with Sonia was gone forever. The world was a harsh, brutal, savage, unfair place where the hopes and dreams of ordinary black men like himself were crushed by a society that worked to keep him in his place. He might not be a genius, but Sonia was right, he had the brains that in another time, another place, could have got him to far greater heights than that of a mini-cab driver. At school he had seen the dreams of able black friends destroyed by a system that labelled them fit only for the dole, factory, or street corner. So much talent blown away. He despised all those wasted years he had spent working in pointless jobs for bosses who looked at him as though he was a form of life one step up from a dog. Every day, as he cruised the streets, he saw too many hopeless, soul-destroyed youths who burned with an undirected, uncontrollable rage. The living dead of a damned generation. The going-nowhere victims of a society, whose power to destroy minds, was stronger than that of any known obeah.

The cop killer knew his own rage would never leave him, it just seemed to grow stronger every day. He refused to allow it to eat into his soul like the cancer that took his father. Instead, the anger would drive him on to both avenge his mother and strike fear into the beast that turned him into the living dead.

His own life was now of little importance. He had no parents to try and do his best for. He had no woman and kids who would bawl at his graveside, and he had no dreams left.

He wondered if his father was watching him now, whether he would understand. Yeah, he probably would. There was a man who believed in playing the last hand. He remembered that even in his final days, as the Grim Reaper knocked hard on his father's door, the old man faced death squarely and said: "cho'!" The memory was crystal clear. He saw the old man smoking away and knocking back a full glass of Bajan rum in his death bed, as Verone Baker remonstrated with him.

"Woman, I don't like to take quotations from a dead fascist but as Mussolini said, 'Man, it bettah to live a day as a lion, than a lifetime as a sheep,' " Lloyd's father said in his broad Bajan accent to his worried wife.

Now Mama rested, without peace, in a grave next to her husband. Maybe, she was better off...

The quaking, hoarse tones of Buju Banton's voice brought him back to the here and now. The rude bwoy in the black BeEm opposite was giving his crew a graphic demonstration of the amplification powers of the car's hi-fi.

The cop killer looked at the A to Z and started the car. He looked at the address on the piece of paper, then at the face of the man in the newspaper cutting. He pulled out onto Kingsland High Road and headed south.

SEVEN

The stiffness in his neck was an uncomfortable way to start the day and the coldness in his limbs heightened the feeling of discomfort. The windows of the Sierra were clouded with water vapour from his breath and small puddles of water had formed on the dashboard, where it had slowly trickled down the windscreen during the night. A half-eaten tuna bagel rested on the dash.

Lloyd yawned a long deep yawn and stretched, to bring life back to his half-dead limbs. He rubbed the sleep from his eyes and tried to take in the time and the setting. The car's clock said 6:30am. As his hand wiped the misted side window, he could see a milkman leaving bottles on the doorstep and removing the empties.

A regular Croydon semi-detached world was starting to come to life outside the confines of his damp and cold, plastic and velour world. Briefcases were being deposited into company cars, the self-employed were loading the tools of their trade into Transit and Escort vans. The sun was already rising.

Forsham Road was already witnessing the ever-increasing stream of early morning rush hour traffic hurtling past the neat, middle-income houses. A wide, busy, main commuting artery, the houses on Forsham Road, with their small front gardens and garages, were set back a small distance from the road which meant it had been easier for the cop killer to park up and sleep the night in his car without attracting the attention of the neighbours. Although at the time of his 2:00am arrival, it would be unlikely that any of the local residents would have been out of their beds. Now with the early morning bustle it was even more unlikely that his presence would attract any more than normal attention.

He sat and watched number 112 for the next forty five minutes before he saw any signs of life. At 7:15 the reason for his vigil appeared at the front door. The man walked to the grey Ford XR3i and opened the door. Lloyd looked hard at him then at the photograph in the newspaper cutting. He checked his watch and smiled, making a mental note of the time as the XR3i disappeared down the road and the Cop Killer stayed put for another ten minutes, as his eyes took in and registered the layout of the land. His engine warmed up, Lloyd indicated right and pulled out into the morning commuter traffic...

The days passed with no discernable difference between them. Lloyd found himself forgetting what day of the week it was or what he had done the day before. The days, and often the nights, were spent on the road taking one fare here and someone else there. One journey became the same as the last one and the face of one punter merged into the face of another.

In the evenings he stayed in or worked. When he retired to his flat his time was spent working with the weights or reading all kinds of books and magazines. This day he would read Victor Headley's 'Yardie', the next a book on explosives or one on philosophy. Every morning and evening the cop killer worked at tuning his mind and making his body fit for the task at hand. His muscles grew stronger and he could now eject the empty magazine from the Colt and insert a fresh one in a few seconds.

His newspaper cuttings, of the injustices perpetuated on ordinary people by the enforcers of law and order, grew each day. The notice board had become too small to accommodate all the data and the neatly cut articles had spilled over onto the wall. The Guardian and The Inquirer provided a good source for his research and he read them eagerly everyday to locate his material. Nails served as his method of securing the clipping to the wall.

The lounge became a shrine to his mission. Near the large windows his weights and bars were carefully positioned. On the table an A4 note paid, red felt pen, biro, scissors, and sellotape were regimentally laid out. Notes and plans were made and kept in a green folder, which also contained paper work relating to his mother's inquest, the Inspector's trial, and various letters from the Metropolitan Police, solicitors, and the 'Justice For Verone Baker Campaign Group'.

At Swift Cars he had worked hard enough in the last two weeks to make sure that the possibility of his dismissal was removed. No one mentioned the incident with Tunde and Sanjay was his usual worried and unsmiling self.

The Colt .45 was kept in a constant state of readiness. Every few days he would make sure the moving parts were still functioning and properly cleaned and lubricated. He had bought a leather shoulder holster for the weapon, which sat the Colt underneath his left armpit. The weapon was better concealed underneath a jacket and it was a great deal more comfortable than when he carried the gun in his waist band. The owner of the Streatham gun shop had looked very uneasy when he had purchased it, but that was the guy's problem, Lloyd reasoned.

He'd not written any more letters to Jackie Spencer but he planned to put pen to paper as soon as the next part of his plan was implemented. He had visited Stockwell, Wanstead and Croydon on several night-time reconnaissance missions and had made notes and plans.

Phillip was back from Jamaica and had called round

his brother's yard twice, but on both occasions Lloyd had been out working. He was looking forward to seeing his brother again and reasoning some more with him. His mind was more focused than before and he hoped he could better explain to Phillip the way things were. He knew they were very different, but he hoped that in these likely last days that there could be a synergy of souls and a better understanding of each other.

Phillip had always been an ambitious, determined to get on in life, sort of guy, while Lloyd had been happier to drift along in a slightly indifferent laid-back kind of way. When they went raving, Phillip always ended up chatting with the girls, while Lloyd had been happier watching the scene from the bar with a beer in his hand. Phillip was the sharp dresser, while Lloyd was happiest in a pair of jeans. Lloyd had been closer to his father —they both had practical, mechanical-orientated minds —whilst Phillip was the apple of his mother's eye. Lloyd was happy in his own company while his brother was more sociable. Lloyd moved out of Navarino Street when he was twenty because he wanted his own space. Phillip, on the other hand, would probably have stayed at home until he married Sharron. Yes, they were like chalk and cheese.

"Michelle in Dalston has, I think, got a few thoughts on this issue. Michelle step forward yah."

"Hello Mikey. I think that ganja should be legalised and people should be free to smoke it in public. It's no more harmful than tobacco and that's legit so why not ganja? Free up de herb!"

"Well, really an' truly, I couldn't agree wid yuh more, Michelle... Dis one goin' out to all ah oonu dat search fe inspiration, from de weed of wisdom. Seek an' ye shall find...Top Cat, an' 'Bun Up De Sensi'."

The cop killer nodded in agreement as he listened to

the opinions expressed on Ruffneck FM and rested his spliff in the ashtray. He took up the hacksaw blade again. A couple more movements and the piece of copper piping dropped to the floor. He examined his handiwork and rested the six-inch piece of tubing on the table with its eight, similarly-sized companions.

The local DIY store was proving to be a handy source of materials for the cop killer in his activities. The blue nylon rope which held 'Cockney Wanker' concealed in his watery grave had come from the shop. So too had the lengths of 22mm copper piping and the brass plumbing fitments.

With a file he now set to work smoothing the rough hacksawed ends of the six inch tubes. Once done, he fitted the brass, self-sealing end caps to one end of each tube. An adjustable spanner locked the caps in place on the tubes.

Now came the dangerous part of the operation. With a steady hand, the cop killer filled each tube with the weedkiller powder and sugar mixture he had prepared earlier. Using a plastic funnel, he poured the powder into each of the tubes until they were full. The powder was carefully compressed, little by little using a rounded length of wood. Then he placed the circular piece of cardboard on top of the compressed powder and with a brass end cap sealed the powder. He drilled the last end cap for the final tube with a small hole. Once the tube had been filled and sealed, he inserted a home made detonator using the components from an oil lamp, firework and pistol ammunition cartridge, into the hole. Some glue sealed it in place. It was the classic home made bomb, perfected from his improvised explosives book.

He was about to tape the tubes together when a knock at the door halted the proceedings. In a flurry of activity he moved the components into a small cardboard box and blew the metal filings off the table top. With the box concealed in a kitchen cupboard, he opened the front door. A sixth sense told him who to expect.

"Come on, open up Mr Baker, this is the police!"

As he walked to the door he gave his reply.

"Babylon, kiss me raas! You'll never take me alive! Yuh wan' tes' me, well step right in and take some licks!" He opened the door. "You took your time tracking me down officer. Fancy a beer?"

Phillip Baker touched fists with his brother and walked into the flat. It was a joke, that to most other people would have seemed in sick taste, but for the brothers it was a way of dealing with the tragedy that had changed their lives.

"Bwoy, I thought I'd come back looking fitter than you," Phillip complemented his brother on his new toned-up physique. "You look in good shape man. What, you been pumping the iron?" he asked looking at the weights by the windows.

"Yeah Phil, trying to keep mind and body together for when they're needed. Stupid question, but did you have a good time out in JA?"

"Oh man, it was mellow, strickly irie an' dem kinda vibes, y'know. Apart from the hustlers who tend to harass you more time. I know times is rough out there, but those geezers really piss you off man."

The good, the bad and the ugly sides of Jamaican life were discussed in great detail as the two brothers sat and drank their beers. It was the first time Phillip had gone to the island of his ancestors and he had returned with a wide range of perceptions and observations. It had been different from what he had expected but an amazing experience all the same.

"I'll tell you something, big brother, I didn't think I'd say. I'm glad to be back in this country, though. I really know now what the expression, 'black British' means. Over here we think we're all Caribbeans, and you get all

98

these geezers with the yellow, green and black all over their motors, but most of them couldn't survive out there. It would be like going to another world. It really is a very different culture over there. It made me realise that we'd better stop looking to the Caribbean as if it's home and one day we're going back. That ain't going to happen. Yeah, we all love chat patois and that's a good thing, not just because it ties us down to our culture, but because more time its needed when you don't want the 'other' man to understand wha' ah gwan, seen? But really and truly when it comes to emigrating back, we couldn't put up with some of the harsh realities of life over there. We gotta start demanding a lot more from this country, and the way this country treats us. There ain't no fuckin' escape route to some other country. This is our country. All these people who go round calling themselves Jamaicans, when they was born up in Hackney Hospital, need to get with the programme. As far as I'm concerned we're black British, and white man and black man had better wake up to that reality."

Phillip spoke with a passion that Lloyd had rarely witnessed and he was impressed with his brother's concern. In the past he was more used to Phillip talking about the best ways to invest your money or the new car he was going to get when he graduated. 'Bwoy, Jamaica must have lick him hard first time,' Lloyd thought to himself.

"Phew Phillip, that's some serious issues you're dealing with." He walked over to the ashtray and re-lit his spliff. "I agree with a lot of what you say. It's important to know your past, but you also have to know where you are at the present. Ours is the in-between generation. Our parents knew they were Caribbeans or Africans, but what about us? Our lot ain't too sure where we belong, here or there. Maybe our children and their children will think of themselves as truly being black British. Maybe the white man will have accepted it by then too. I doubt it, but you never know."

They talked for some time about issues surrounding the 'black experience'. Towards the end of the evening Phillip's face looked pensive and deep in thought.

"Listen Lloyd, I don't know if there's any truth in this or not. An old long time spar of mine said, while I was away he'd heard that a yout' I used to know, Michael Watts, told the police that I was dealing in crack, and that's why they went to the house."

Lloyd's face was sullen and serious. When he spoke, his voice was quiet and deliberate.

"How did your mate hear this information?" He concentrated intensely on his brother's reply.

"This guy, Michael Watts, apparently told his girlfriend this, and the girl then told her best friend Diane, who is my spar's sister. The story is that he told the cops this to get them off his back."

"Who is this Michael Watts?"

"He was one of the loafters at Hackney College when I was doing my A-levels. He started dealing after college and was always on the frontline in the old days before the cops shut it down."

Phillip sounded troubled. Lloyd knew what was going on his mind, but didn't want to say anything until his brother mentioned it.

"I hope you don't think it was my fault that mum got killed. He came by our house once, but he was no friend of mine. I hardly knew him... He was just someone at college. I..."

Lloyd cut him short.

"Phillip, easy nuh. Of course it's not your fault. Don't even think such foolishness."

Phillip still looked troubled.

"Look Lloyd, I'll find Michael Watts and somehow, I'll make him pay."

"Phillip, keep well away from the geezer. Let me deal with things. I'll reason with him and find out what really went down? Don't worry, leave it to me."

Whatever happened, Lloyd didn't want his younger brother involved. Nothing should come in the way of Phillip's career. Phillip finally agreed to allow Lloyd to take care of the business.

"Nice. Now tell me where this Michael Watts hangs."

"I don't know exactly. He's a Hackney yout'. I see him around all the time. You can't miss his car. A purple Vauxhall Astra GTE convertible, white roof, wide alloys, and white lettering on the sides saying 'The GTE Touch'. On Fridays and Saturdays he usually hangs out at one of the night clubs on Kingsland High Road, dealing."

Lloyd was deep in thought. Suddenly the incident with the young guy weeks ago at the Ridley Road bakery came back to him. The image of the purple Astra GTE was clear in his mind...

He had planned it as thoroughly as one could plan something that would happen in a public place. The bins were in place, the concrete block at the right spot. It was a set up he had spent weeks thinking about every possibility and had worked out a series of escape routes where he could flee on foot and where police cars couldn't follow. Sunday had been chosen as the day of operation because the cop killer figured that it was the day of the week when at two o'clock in the morning everyone would be in their beds.

The Gillsmore Estate in south London's Stockwell area was a notorious 'problem' council housing estate, made up of four-storey, 1930's-built tenement flats. Walkways ran along each floor and the flats were unusual in that one block of flats was joined to another by a connecting walkway. This provided residents with an almost infinite variety of ways to exit from the estate, and it also provided the cop killer with a large number of options to avoid capture.

Many flats on the estate were boarded up and the local council had plans to demolish the blocks, which had a reputation for being a haven for squatters and an area of widespread drugs dealing.

He knew of the estate, having passed it countless times, and having dropped a number of fares there over the years at Swift Cars. It had all the right ingredients for his simple, but brutally effective, assault plan and the labyrinth of nearby, bollard-blocked, no through roads, was ideal.

His clothing had been chosen with thought for the mission. The dark blue track suit and black trainers gave him concealment in the dark, and advantage in any sprint, and if it was necessary to run he hoped that a man out running in a track suit at night would attract less suspicion.

He had taken the precaution of tying lengths of rope across the rails on some of the stairs leading up from the yard to the flats. Behind the rope he had placed rubbish-filled bin bags. While it was not a substantial barrier for anyone who might try and rush up the stairs leading from the yard to the flat walkways, it would slow a pursuing cop sufficiently to give the cop killer vital extra seconds for escape.

Once again the cop killer checked out his surroundings. All stations were go. All he needed to do was to switch on the torch in the bin room and phone the police. He walked down the stairs, carefully stepping over the ropes, and walked to the side road next to the flats. As he had checked earlier, the pay phone was working. He dialled 999.

"Hello. Yeah, can I have the police please." His old man, cockney voice sounded very convincing, especially over a phone.

"Yeah, I wonder san if you could send a car to the back of Osbourne House on The Gillsmore Estate, Stockwell Road. There's a bleedin' youngster messin' about wiv the cars in the yard. He's got a torch and I just saw 'im go into the bin room just as you drive into the yard."

"My name? Sidney Harper I live at number 72."

The cop killer legged it back to the bin room and flicked on the torch, resting it on the floor at the back of the room, its beam shining up at the ceiling. Next he moved quickly up the stairs to his position on the third floor. The section of balcony he now occupied directly overlooked the entrance to the bin room. Most of the flats on the floor were boarded up and he was unlikely to be disturbed by any nearby tenants. With his gloved hands, he lifted the large slab of concrete onto the brick wall that ran along the edge of the walkways and positioned it carefully. About two feet in length and about 12 inches wide, he had stored it in the boot of his car since removing it from the Matthew's factory in Hackney. Now its time had come to be put into service. It was unconventional, but in a battle to the death you don't go by the rule book. He adjusted the woolly hat on his head and waited.

"What you doing mate?"

He had not heard their approach and was startled by the voice. As he turned, his hand instinctively reached for the 'matic concealed in its holster under his track suit top. He caught sight of the youths before his hand had reached inside the fleecy lining.

On first sight he had assumed the youngsters were black. In the darkness and with their sweat shirt hoods up he had not seen their faces. The ragga-style baggy slash-cut jeans, high top trainers and the deliberate swagger in their walk, gave them the appearance of local homeboys. As they approached and held their heads up, he could see

103

they were aged around fourteen and white. The cop killer was relieved to see them.

"Bloody hell. You kids gave me a right fright. I thought you was the radics."

The taller one did most of the talking.

"No way, mate. We spend most of our time duckin' from the old bill." Luckily for Lloyd, like most kids in high-crime areas the two boys viewed the police as a threat. The youngster looked curiously at the concrete block perched on the brick wall.

"What ya got that for? What ya doin' then?"

The cop killer smiled at the two kids and spoke in a Jack Nicholson-style American accent.

"What we have here gentlemen, is a total lack of respect for law and order. Using this here projectile I intend to strike a blow, no jest intended, for all oppressed people everywhere."

The youngsters looked at each other uneasily, unsure whether the man was mad or joking. Again the taller one spoke.

"Yeah? Sounds like a wicked idea man. Mind if we chill here for a moment?"

The cop killer heard a car approaching and prepared himself. As the two cops got out of the squad car and started walking towards the lit-up bin room, the cop killer whispered to the youngsters.

"Get the fuck out of here! Start running."

The boys didn't need to be told twice.

Everything happened at once. The cop killer gripped the block of concrete in both hands and held it over the edge of the balcony just as the cops walked to the bin room's entrance. He felt like a bomber plane crewman in one of those old World War Two movies. Just as the guy would line up his bomb sight before releasing his deadly pay load, the cop killer lined up the block with his eye, trying to gauge its likely target. The first cop walked into the killing zone just as the youngsters were running along the centre section of the walkway. The cops turned to see who was running.

"Gotcha!" Lloyd muttered to himself as his hands released their burden.

Whether it was luck or expert judgement, the results were viciously effective Like a steam hammer, the concrete bomb plummeted downwards with more than the required velocity. It struck the first cop with such ferocious impact on his head and neck that a piece of scalp and skull were wrenched from his head. It was like some primitive execution device; the death was horrifying and instant.

From above, Lloyd saw the impact and the cop crumple like a pack of cards. The sound was frighteningly loud — like a stone cracking open the shell of a dry coconut. He didn't stop to savour the moment. He turned and fled down some side stairs into another block, then across a yard and out into a side road. The weeks of physical training now reaped their rewards. The wave of adrenaline washing through his body also played its part. His legs moved with such swiftness, that they felt as though they belonged to a champion sprinter.

From street to alleyway, to street, he ran like a shadow in the dark. His heart pumped like the pistons in a racing car's engine and he gulped for air as he dashed down the yellow-lit, back routes of Stockwell. The Colt jolted backwards and forwards underneath his arm. He had played it safe and parked the Sierra some way from the flats; now he was rapidly approaching the side street. He slowed down to a jog and turned to see if he was being pursued. There was no one. The jog became a walk as he turned the corner and then a stroll, as he approached the car and jumped in. He started the Ford and headed northwards. Suddenly he burst into an uncontrollable fit of laughter, a delayed release of the terrifying fear that now seemed to overwhelm him.

He knew he had cried havoc and let slip the dogs of war. There was definitely no turning back now. He smoked a cigarette as he approached Elephant & Castle and knew that ten minutes ago, he just became the most wanted man in London.

EIGHT

Wesley Banfield looked down at the papers on his desk. His left thumb and forefinger alternated between slowly rubbing his greying beard and adjusting the glasses resting on his nose. He was clearly giving the matter a great deal of deliberation.

A scholarly-looking Jamaican in his early forties, Banfield looked and carried himself like a man ten years his senior. His suits were smart but out of date and his conservative look and manner had earned him the nickname of 'Papa Doc' from the Inquirer's staff. He had been the newspaper's Editor for the last six years, having joined from the BBC's Caribbean World Service radio department.

"My dear, whether the man is a deranged lunatic, or indeed a policeman's killer, is of little consequence to the issue at hand." His words were slow and thought out, rather like a professor delivering a lecture. His pronunciation was middle-class Jamaican.

"The paper would look dyam foolish if we printed a story about some man who claims to be busy licking down half of the Metropolitan Police Force. Jackie, where is the proof? What evidence has this man supplied to back up his claims? He even takes credit for killing some police motorcyclist in an incident the Force themselves are treating as an accident...! Let me ask you somet'ing? If a man walk off Brixton High Road and come in here claiming to be the Son of God, yuh gwan print his story?"

Jackie Spencer reflected on the matter and concluded that her boss was right.

"Yeah, point taken Wesley. It's just that this Stockwell

107

thing is front page news in all the nationals. It would be nice if we could have our own little twist on the story, but fair enough."

The Editor had one other point to add:

"In all the reports I've read, it stated that police believe children are involved. The other policeman in the attack says he saw two youngsters, who he believed were black, running from the scene. So where does our man come into this?"

Jackie was disappointed but that was journalism. Whenever it seemed as though a potential scoop came into her grasp, it always seemed to vanish like sand through her fingers. She headed out of the Editor's office and got on with the mundane...

Here is something you can't understand...
How I could just kill man.
Here Is something you can't understand...
How I could just kill man.

All day long, the cop killer had been listening to music so ruff, tuff, hard and loud it couldn't be played on legal radio, no way. But this wasn't legal, it was Ruffneck FM style and they were outlaws because they played the records people wanted to hear.

Streaks of rain slithered across the windscreen before the wiper blades cut their trickle short. The gradual onset of winter was heralded by the October afternoon sky, which slowly turned a darker shade of grey, as the sun bid its leave of absence. The drizzle was rapidly becoming a downpour. Lloyd stared blankly at the bustle of commuters, making good their escape from their nine-to-five prisons. Farringdon Road was solid. Pure gridlock worries. He was in no mood for conversation but his passenger had other ideas.

"What a fackin' way to go, eh? Eh?!"

Lloyd looked up at the rear view mirror, uncertain if the comment was a criticism of his chosen route to the South Bank. He awaited further clarification.

"They say it's fackin' kids that done it, eh? Eh? Fackin' kids. Can you believe it, eh? I tell you the fackin' world's goin' fackin' down the pan. What a terrible way to die. They say his skull was cracked clean open. Eh? Terrible way to die. Course, I blame it on society. Society's gone fackin' soft on 'em, eh? Eh? I'd fackin' like to get my fackin' hands on some of 'em, wring their fackin' necks for 'em. Eh? I was in fackin' Aden serving my fackin' country when I was their age. Course National Service was the fackin' best thing that ever happened to this country. Eh? Gave me discipline. Fackin' respect for other people, eh? Eh? If you ask me, it's the fackin' loony left mate, eh? Fackin' lesbians and pooftahs running the education system. I tell you, in my day, if we ever caught hold of some pooftah we'd have given him a fackin' good hiding. Eh, eh? Nowadays they'll giv' em a fackin' council grant. Can you adam and eve it? Eh?"

The old man was reading an article in The Sun detailing the arguments why policemen should be armed. A genuine, hundred percent white trash bigot, thought Lloyd, as he listened to the pensioner's solutions to the ills of society.

"Maybe the Old Bill should be issued with stronger helmets in case of similar attacks." Lloyd offered, irritated by the traffic and the old man. The sarcasm had an aggressive tone which was lost on the passenger.

"Nah sunshine, it was a fackin' block a concrete 'it em. They had it on the news. No fackin' helmet's gonna save you from that."

"You know old man, you're probably right there. But they'd better do something to protect themselves, cause there's gonna be a whole heap ah bacon frying in the old town tonight. You know what I mean... sunshine?"

The old man didn't know what he meant, but he could tell from the way it was said that it was best he kept quiet. He concentrated on his newspaper. Lloyd kissed his teeth at his passenger's reflection in the rear-view mirror.

It was a relief to get the old man out of the Sierra and an even greater relief that he was not working that evening. He could head home and chill out. It was Friday and that was a good enough reason to treat himself to a curried goat, rice and peas take-away.

Today was the first day since Sunday night that he had woken up and not thought that the radics would come busting through his door. He'd still slept fully-clothed and with his 'matic cocked under the pillow, but the fear of imminent arrest had subsided. He had wondered how long it would be before the youths were located, but as everyone was assuming they were black, it might be some time. If the kids kept their mouths shut it might never happen. He began humming the lyrics of an old reggae tune which decried the fact that whenever there was a crime, "de yard man get de blame." For once, the injustice of the system was working in his favour.

"Is there always gonna be, one more bridge to cross.
Is there always gonna be, one more bridge to cross.
Everyday, all I can see is a brother 'gainst a brother,
A brother against a brother, I would say...
Too much confusion, y'all.
I can't tek it no more inna Babylon, inna Babylon.
I'll be going on de first train tomorrow,
Don't need no pain or sorrow..."

The wailing tones of Big Youth pulsated from the car's stereo as darkness descended on the rain-washed streets of the capital. The beams of a hundred car head lights reflected off the glistening Whitechapel Road. The traffic was moving with a little more urgency and it wasn't long before the blue Sierra was passing Bethnal Green tube station and cruising up Hackney's Mare Street. Another ten minutes and Lloyd was parking up outside the Sam's Caribbean take away on Chatsworth Road.

"Yeah, man. Babylon tek a serious lick so. Me seh, sooner or later, judgement day haffe come, star. 'As ye sew, so shall ye reap'. Ah dat my Bible seh. Dem bloodclaat babylon lick down nuff yout' a'ready. Now dem time come fe true, star. Dem time come."

The old rasta was in deep debate with the middle-aged man serving behind the counter when the cop killer entered. Everywhere he had gone this week the topic of the Stockwell killing seemed to be the issue of discussion.

The undertone of much of the media reporting had a distinctly racial bias. The tabloid press had seized on the quote from Scotland Yard which said that the colleague of the murdered officer thought he saw two black youngsters running away from the scene laughing. By the time it had appeared in the press, the possibility had become a fact. One newspaper had even come up with the headline. 'YARDIE PROBE OVER COP MURDER'. The story quoted an unnamed police source, saying that detectives were examining a possible link between drug dealers in the area and the killing.

The incident was being widely discussed in the black community and there were many who shared the views of the old lion dread.

The man behind the counter cut short his conversation to serve Lloyd. There was no curry today, so he settled for some jerk chicken, rice and peas, plantain and a dumpling. And a bottle of Dragon to go would help wash things down nice...

The plate washed and the food containers deposited in

the dustbin, the Cop Killer sat down to build up a smoke of sensi. He looked at the near empty bag of herb and realised he had been smoking copious amounts of ganja recently. He had paid quite a few visits to Herbsman in Brixton and had been buying larger and larger quantities each time.

The lounge wall was now almost half covered with newspaper cuttings, the Stockwell killing adding greatly to his collection. He wondered when Jackie Spencer would write up his story. Maybe she didn't believe his letters? Never mind. Soon he would be able to give her all the proof she needed, he thought.

Drawing up increasingly elaborate plans and writing notes had become a daily ritual. He had contemplated a suicide-style mission on a police station where he had pictured himself storming the station and going out with his gun blasting. A brief moment of glory had a nihilistic attraction, but he reasoned that a gradual war of attrition would be more effective in the long run. If his luck held out he could have a reasonable run for his money, he figured. There was still a whole heap of unfinished business for him to sort out. He looked at his watch. It would soon be time for him to go back into combat...

"If loving you was a crime,
I'd be in prison long time, I ah tell you."

"Yes, indeed dat's how me feel when me spy dem nice-nice gyal up Dalston way... Moving in nice an' easy in a lover's revival style for all the ladies out there. You're listening to the Smooth Operator, Robbie Mac, on the Station with Vibration, Ruffneck FM... Remember, if yuh cyan stand de heat, keep out of de mixin' and blendin'.... Tonight's burning topic on discussion is: Are the ladies getting too slack...? Now remember Francis from Edmonton? He reckoned that too many gyal, ah

too quick to drop dem panty. A back to basic values, de man ah call for. What's your opinion ladies? Don't sit and moan, get 'pon de phone, and call Ruffneck FM... The place where rude bwoys do it rrrrruffer!"

He slowed the car down to a crawl and carefully scanned the long line of cars parked up on the right. He turned the radio down so it wouldn't disturb his concentration. BMW, Escort, Audi, Renault 19, Nissan. One by one he checked them out.

A group of criss looking girls who'd just climbed out of a VW threw hostile stares at him as he cruised by. The Sierra's slow speed gave the driver the appearance of a curb crawler and they weren't pleased.

Outside the large neon-lit club, a crowd of ravers were patiently waiting to pass the scrutinising eyes of the burly bouncers standing at the door. The booming, distorted sound of the music system could be heard in the confines of the car. The Belview Club was one of the many nightclubs frequented exclusively by black ravers — couples and singles — who felt comfortable to show off their latest fashions with impunity in its elegant surroundings. Located in the middle of an industrial estate near Hackney Marshes, there were no neighbours to complain about the deafening volume at which the music was played non-stop at weekends.

The crowds had come in their thousands tonight. Vincent Irie, the latest lover's sensation, was over from Jamaica to perform his first UK concert. Many of his female fans were there, accompanied by partners who looked like they had little choice in the matter. Because the only way to reach the venue was by car, the approach road was packed tight with every conceivable form of transport from flash German sports cars to pick-up trucks.

The cop killer lit another cigarette and increased his

speed. He had been driving frantically all evening, like a psycho with his windows rolled down. He had drawn another blank at Belview and decided to head back to Stokey and check out the situation up there. He was getting bored and needed to find something else to get into after several hours cruising the streets of Hackney without seeing what he wanted. He had driven past every club in the area but he'd had no success.

The endless crowds of ravers, raggas, mampies, yardies, soul heads, bad bwoys, nice gyals, wannabes, and wasters gave Lloyd a feeling of isolation. While he sat in his own mobile world there was another world happening out there and it looked like they were having fun. It was a Friday night and apart from him, everyone seemed to be out to rave.

"You can't run away from yourself," the cop killer said out loud to himself. He put the bottle of Thunderbird to his lips and took another mouthful of the brew.

A combination of frustration, herb and alcohol was getting him in a belligerent mood. At the traffic lights he secured the screw cap on the bottle and threw it on the passenger seat. He again passed the small club, Vibes, on Daubeny Road but again it was a wasted visit.

He returned the stare of a big built guy with a shaved head, who was leaning against the black painted wall outside. The traffic moved on, and their eye-to-eye sparring was broken up. The Sierra was several hundred yards away and the club had disappeared out of sight. The cop killer studied his own reflection in the rear-view mirror and muttered to himself in a vexed tone that alternated between an American and a Jamaican accent.

"What you looking at, motherfucker...? Yuh fucking bawl head pussyclaat, yuh... You come here and fuckin' stare... You motherfucker... Fucking motherfucker. Come here and I'll fucking blow you away. Motherfucker. Cho', If you're man enough, den come test me."

He headed towards Dalston on his circuit run before heading back towards Hackney again. The time was approaching 3:00 am. He finished off the last of the Thunderbird and tossed the bottle out of the window.

He had made up his mind to cancel the night's operation, but decided on one more pass by Ramones on the Upper Clapton Road. As he lit his last Benson & Hedges he caught sight of his elusive goal. His heart beat a little quicker, as his eyes made the confirmation.

Thre was a purple Vauxhall Astra GTE convertible with white roof and White vinyl lettering on the side: 'The GTE Touch'. It was parked near the traffic lights at the roundabout and about 100 feet from the club. He couldn't be a hundred percent certain, but was sure that the guy standing at the railings by the Astra, was the same one he'd knocked shoulders with at the Ridley Road Bakery.

He indicated left at the roundabout and turned down Kenninghall Road. He parked the car further down the road, then took the Colt from its holster under the driver's seat. Tucking it into the waist at the back of his black jeans, he adjusted the position of the weapon and checked that the jacket covered it properly.

As he hurried back towards the club, he had no sensation of nervousness as he'd felt at the flats in Stockwell. He felt relaxed but very charged. A sense that he was not totally in touch with his mind or body was pervasive. In a strange way he felt happy, as if he was reaching the end of his travels and was looking forward to finishing the long and tiring journey.

As he moved swiftly in the damp night air his step gradually increased and he felt powerful. The coldness of the gun's steel permeated his cotton T-shirt and he became aware of the weapon's weight at the back of his jeans. The .45 was primed and the safety catch was in the 'off' position.

Closer and closer he came and now he could see the

guy chatting with another man and a woman on the pavement near the car. The Astra's owner wore his hair cropped with tram lines at the right side. His baggy jeans were a mustard and green colour. His leather jacket, black in colour. The girl handed him some money and he passed something back to her. It was too dark for the cop killer to see that clearly, but he knew what it was. A dope man always had plenty of product. He was now about fifteen feet away from the group.

"Michael, wha'ppen? Long time, boss."

Michael Watts broke off his conversation to see who the acquaintance was. He studied the cop killer's features trying to place his smiling face.

"So Michael, ah yahso yuh deh? Still selling crack to de pickney?"

The couple were puzzled too. They looked at the smiling cop killer then at Michael Watts. Was this a friend? What sort of joke was it to broadcast his business all over the place? The questions raced through their minds. Watts was equally baffled.

"Me know you, star?"

The humble tone of the enquiry indicated Watts' unease and confusion with the situation. The cop killer ignored his question but moved in closer instead.

"So Mikey, dem seh dat the crack an' cocaine ah destroying the black yout'. What is your view on this very important issue?"

The couple sensed trouble and started backing away. Watts remained puzzled.

"Where me know you from, star?"

The cop killer reached behind his back and stepped a pace closer keeping his finger on the trigger.

"Mikey, yuh nuh know me, but maybe in hell, we might 'ave ah longer time to get acquainted."

A squirt of blood flew onto the woman's face as she and her man turned to flee. A flash of flame shot from the

116

muzzle of the gun, as Watts was knocked back onto the metal railings. The cop killer had aimed at his chest but the first bullet made impact in the side of his neck, sending a long jet of blood bursting from the gaping wound. He squeezed the trigger and let fly another bullet and another and another. In the split seconds that the dope man rested against his metal prop, a volley of three or four shots tore into his body.

Watts was on his back, at that moment still alive. The fearsome recoil of the powerful .45 and Lloyd's lack of experience with firearms, had caused the bullets to strike at random parts of Watts' body; none of the shots were instantly fatal. He lay in a growing red puddle on the wet, cold pavement. His eyes blinked rapidly and the fingers on his left hand, which were bloodied and dirty from the ground, twitched vigorously. Lloyd took two steps forward and knelt over the dying man.

"Remember Verone Baker? You sent the 'radication squad to her house and she was killed. You know how it go, star, a life for a life... Good night Michael."

The cop killer's words were soft and like those of a mother biding her child a restful sleep.

He rested the muzzle of the pistol on Watts' forehead, looked away, then pulled the trigger.

NINE

The light but consistent drizzle showed no signs of
quitting and the grey, depressing sky had been a
permanent feature from morning. He watched the
rain spray from the fast moving cars turn into a mist as
the wind blew across the bleak concrete landscape. The
cop killer stared out through the misty windows of his
flat, far away into the distance, his mind further away. He
had been standing there for ten minutes, his soul locked
in a kind of deep hypnotic trance.

"Revolution has come,
Time to pick up the gun... okay."

The beat belonged to that of a kicking hip hop tune
and the lyrics passed through the empty doors of his
conscious into his sub-conscious being. He snapped out of
it and listened to the chorus which had the voice of
Malcolm X mixed into the fast pulsing beat:

"We're tired of being used, of being abused.
We assert our right to defend ourselves,
by any means necessary...!"

"Revolution has come,
Time to pick up the gun... okay."

He walked to the sofa and started going through the
newspapers. He could find nothing about the Stockwell
attack. The police were still dragging in scores of local
black youngsters for questioning but were getting

nowhere in their murder inquiry. A week ago the Met's Commissioner had gone on local television and slagged off the Estate's residents who, he said, had been "uncooperative" and explained that not a single witness had come forward from the Estate.

When heavy saturation policing in the neighbourhood failed to bear fruit, despite giving the impression that they were hunting down an assassin who had gunned down the Queen, the media lost interest. It was obvious to them that there weren't going to be any quick arrests. Two days after Stockwell, when a senior Tory minister resigned after being exposed as part of a bestial sex ring, the media's focus shifted totally away from the killing. Nevertheless, the cop killer decided to play smart by laying low to breathe a while. He posed a problem the police really couldn't sleep off, and it was essential that he stayed alive as long as possible.

The Michael Watts shooting had, like so many young black male murders, been written off by the police as "probably drugs related". It received some coverage in the Hackney Gazette and on the local radio and TV, but it was ignored by many nationals and those that did cover it relegated it to a small one-column story. Once again there had been a total lack of witnesses to the shooting. Even the woman, who was taken to Homerton Hospital covered in the victim's blood and suffering from shock, claimed not to have seen the man who pulled the trigger.

After administering the last rites on Watts, the blood-soaked cop killer had strolled away calmly while crowds of clubgoers fled the scene. He had simply climbed into his car and driven away. During the police questioning of the crowd standing outside the club, 240 witnesses claimed they didn't see anything, as they were inside the tiny, nearby pattie shop at the time.

There was nothing of interest in the newspapers so he deposited them in the kitchen bin and made himself a coffee. He looked at his watch then re-read the note on the table:

Dear Lloyd,
Called round this evening but, surprise-surprise, you weren't in. Will call round tomorrow at 4:00pm. We need to talk so if you're not working, be there! We've got important things to discuss.
Respeck.
Phillip.
PS. When are you going to get a phone?!!!!!!!!

He went back to the window and once more slipped into a trance. When there was a knock at the door he had no idea how long he had been gazing out into the grey wilderness beyond. He looked at his watch but couldn't remember what the time had been when he last looked. It was now 4:30pm

Phillip was smartly dressed in a blue double-breasted suit underneath a grey lightweight coat. He shook the rain off his umbrella in the hallway and stepped into the room then laid down his leather case and mobile phone on the table. The two brothers embraced each other briefly and awkwardly.

"Wha'ppen boss?" Lloyd greeted his brother.

"Yeah alright, you know. Trying to avoid the puddles and the bank manager."

"What, you the accountancy wizard got financial problems, ?"

"Nah, the opposite. The Manager suddenly wants to know me. I've just come from the bank and I'm pleased to inform you Mr Lloyd Baker, that I have just credited your account to the tune of £33,580."

In his whole life Lloyd had rarely sniffed more than £2,000 at any one time in his account, but he seemed unmoved by the news.

"What's that for?"

"It's from the solicitor. Your share from the sale of mum's house. I thought you'd be pleased. Is something wrong?"

For the first time Phillip noticed his brother's sombre mood but wasn't sure how to tackle things. Glancing around the room he noticed also that the number of newspaper cuttings on the wall had grown since he was last there but he was unsure what it all meant.

"No, don't worry Phil, I'm fine man. I'm just tired. I appreciate everything you've done sorting out the legal t'ing. I couldn't have done it without you, man."

Phillip was studying the cuttings on the wall. He came straight out with it.

"Lloyd, you know dem kill Michael Watts last Friday?"

Phillip knew it was a pointless question as he could see the newspaper cutting about the shooting up on the wall, but it was a way to serve notice on his next question.

"Lloyd..." the younger brother began cautiously, "you weren't in any way involved with his death were you?"

Again as he spoke Phillip's eyes realised that the question might be redundant. On the floor, under the table, he could see the small pile of gun magazines.

The cop killer turned and looked his brother straight in the eye.

"The way I look at things Phillip, is that Michael Watts was an informer who killed himself. When he sent those armed assassins to our mother's house, he signed his own death certificate. Is like dem buddhists ah seh, 'bad karma'. The bad things you do in this life shall catch up with you in the same life. Cause an' effect. Understand...? No one will miss Michael Watts. People like him are destroying the black community. Destroying the youts with crack an' cocaine. Because if the youts couldn't get it, nobody would fuck with it. What right does he have to live? Even the cops ain't bothered. He was fuckin' scum.

An' scum deserve what's comin' at 'em."

Phillip looked hard at his brother. He looked fucked up. At that moment he realised how little he understood about what was going on in Lloyd's head. Perhaps he had never understood his loner brother. He decided to play it cool.

"Lloyd, you still didn't answer my question. And you can't come making judgements on people when you're burning weed non-stop."

"Phillip, weed is one t'ing and coke is another. Weed was from creation, found on King Solomon's grave, for the healing of the nation, for wisdom, health an' strength, y'know. But the coke is a different thing, it's escapism and I just reckon we as black people need to deal with the reality of what's goin' on in dis yah time. You live round these parts, man. I don't need to tell you the programme! "

Phillip could see that he wasn't going to get an answer to his question and decided he didn't really want one anyway. Lloyd was right about one thing, thought Phillip, Michael Watts wouldn't be missed. With one bad bwoy gone, another one had already stepped into his shoes.

The main reason for his visit concluded, Phillip decided to make a move. The vibe was not very relaxed and though he feared his brother may have been involved in the dope dealer's execution, he thought it best to let the matter rest. Lloyd had changed a lot in the last fifteen months. He probably needed time to get things together and sort his head out.

"Well Lloyd, gotta chip, man. I said I'd meet Sharron at six. Take care, yuh hear...?"Phillip looked his brother hard in the eyes as he spoke. "Just be cool," he cautioned. "And Lloyd, you should take a break. Use the money to go on holiday, visit Yard or sump'n, man. You need a rest."

"Yeah you're right. Tek it easy my yout'. Respeck."

They touched fists and Lloyd saw his brother to the

door, then returned to the table to make some final written plans for the evening...

It was 7:37pm when he got to Forsham Road, Croydon. The peaceful quiet of the suburban neighbourhood brought back memories to the cop killer of his childhood when London seemed calm like still waters. But the days when children could play on inner city streets were long gone. In comparison with the rough streets of Hackney, Croydon seemed almost quiet. He avoided parking in the same place he'd stopped before, choosing instead to pull up about 50 yards further up. The grey Escort XR3i was outside the house with the curtains drawn and the lights on. He lit a cigarette and thought back to that first uncomfortable night he had spent outside this house, and how cold and stiff he'd felt the next morning. He'd been back to stake out the house another three or four times since then, each time gaining a little more information about Sergeant Keith Summers. He didn't know what role Summers had played in the death of his mother, but he had seen him on the television after the inquest and knew that he was scum. Phillip had sat through every minute of the inquest and told him about Summers. How had Phillip described him? Oh yeah, "pure nastiness" he'd said. Well this was the pay-back. The cop killer was good and ready and equipped to rip shit in a battle. That was what he was there for.

He didn't know enough about the movements of Summers to come up with much of a plan. He would have to watch and wait and then strike when he got the opportunity. It might not be tonight but it would be one night. Sometime when his target stepped out the door to get a take-away, get a video, or a few beers at the offie. Lloyd would bide his time and strike. It was a waiting game and he would be happy to wait until the right time.

At 8:15 the cop killer sat up sharply in his seat. The front door of 112 opened and Sergeant Summers walked out. Instinctively, Lloyd pulled the pistol out of the shoulder holster he always wore when going out on a job and for a moment considered putting some slugs into the cop there and then, but decided against it. The police officer climbed into his XR3i and turned the ignition. His engine started, his headlights on, the cop killer drove off in pursuit of his prey.

He kept his distance, so as to not make it obvious he was following the man. Along the High Street, left at Addinshaw Road, then right. At the next set of traffic lights past Fenshawk Road the cop killer jumped the lights on red to keep his man in touch. The XR3i was going at some speed and when Lloyd was forced to jump another set of lights he came within inches of colliding with a white van approaching the junction from the cross road. They were heading in the direction of Streatham and the cop killer was uncertain whether the Sergeant knew he was being followed. It was difficult on the traffic-filled streets of London to try and keep a discreet distance from someone you were tailing. He hoped that Summers didn't use his mirror too often, for if he did he couldn't have helped noticing the blue Sierra that had been following all the way from Croydon.

The Escort carried on in the direction of Streatham, then turned off Streatham High Road, along Streatham Common North, then left into Valley Road. It seemed a twisting route to take and the cop killer began to suspect that he had been spotted and the element of surprise had been lost. For a moment he considered trying to ram the car off the road then opening fire with the 'matic. No, that would be foolish and likely to end in disaster. He put the idea out of his head and decided to play this hand out.

The XR3i turned down Leigham Court Road and parked at the bottom where it met Streatham High Road.

The cop killer watched the man turn left. He parked up quickly and sprinted down the road after him. As he turned left there was no sign of Summers. He examined the possibilities. There was a pub, a pizza restaurant, and a cinema. He took his chance with the pub.

The Falstaff was packed and noisy, with drinkers supping pints in a haze of cigarette smoke and the droning sound of indistinguishable pop tunes from the juke box and the electronic beeps and whizzes of a handful of fruit machines. The cop killer slowly edged his way round the pub, his eyes scanning discreetly every which way for his prey. He was about to give up the ghost and walk out the door, when he sighted Summers emerging from the gents to join a group of noisy men round a table filled with empty pint glasses and crisp packets. The cop killer looked more closely at the group of men aged in their early to late thirties; it was obvious that they were police officers. The neat, short haircuts and the odd blue shirt underneath a casual jacket made it obvious.

Summers approached the group and said his 'hellos'. A man with a moustache handed him a pint and he sat down to join his mates. The cop killer bought a drink and played the fruit machine, all the time keeping an eye on his prey. Everyone in the pub was too engrossed in their own little drunken world to notice the well-built young black man who had entered alone. It was the perfect place where an observer could remain invisible to everyone else but himself. He had to keep a careful watch on Summers. His eyes firmly on the prize.

Like a die-hard gambler, the cop killer slotted coin after coin into the fruit machine, without pausing to blink. It seemed the more coins he poured into the machine, the more invisible he became. He ordered another drink and carried on the waiting game. When it all seemed too simple, along came the fly in the ointment.

"You got a light, handsome?"

He turned and saw from the glint in her eyes that she wanted more than just her cigarette lit! In her late thirties, she seemed like the kind of white middle-class women who be concerned about environmental issues and like to go to art galleries on a Sunday afternoon. She looked relaxed and very confident. How much of this was due to alcohol, Lloyd wasn't sure. He smiled and handed her his lighter.

"Hi, I'm Sarah," she said offering her hand.

"Lloyd, nice to meet you Sarah."

"So Lloyd, is your life really so sad that you have to come to the pub and play on one of these all night?"

He didn't reply. He could see from her unsteadiness that she was clearly very drunk and he had no intention of troubling it. He looked at his watch as the barman called for last orders.

"So Floyd, what do you do when you're not gambling?"

"The name's Lloyd."

"Oh dear, my apologies. Lloyd, Floyd, what's the difference? What's in a name, eh? ...A rose by any other name...?" Her speech was becoming more slurred as she held on to Lloyd's shoulder to steady himself. This woman could wreck his mission if he wasn't careful, the cop killer thought to himself. He turned to check on Summers. The table was empty.

He dashed out of the pub. The group were nowhere to be seen. He ran back to where Summers had parked his car. It had gone.

Quickly he considered the options open to him. Should he try and check out the High Road? Maybe they had gone off somewhere else for some food? Why would he have taken his car? Was he on his way back home? The cop killer had only one real option open to him. He had to get back to the Sergeant's house as quickly as possible.

He jumped in the Sierra and started up. Slamming down the accelerator, the car's wheels spun on the wet road sending off an acrid cloud of white, rubber smoke. He would have to tear through the traffic to get back to Croydon before Summers. Now he was in his killing zone this fucker was his, he reasoned. Like a crazed bat out of hell, he shot up Leigham Court Road with his speedo touching 60mph. He overtook two cars by zipping into the opposite lane and nearly caused a head-on smash with an oncoming car. The lights were on red but he slowed then turned right, the back end skidding on the wet road. He kept the heat on all the way down Valley Road. At 65mph he passed a police car going the other way, but knew that by the time it had turned round he would have been long gone. Once onto Streatham High Road he darted between the traffic, cutting up a number of irate motorists who angrily flashed their headlights. While slipping down the inside lane of traffic he smashed off the wing mirror of a parked up Mercedes sports. But that didn't stop him. He simply continued driving like a lunatic. He jumped two more red lights while sounding his horn and flashing his lights so that other car drivers would think his was a police car.

As he approached Croydon, at the traffic lights on the High Road, he saw a Grey XR3i ahead of him. He pulled up behind and recognised the number plate. They were only five minutes away from the Sergeant's house. As the lights turned green and the XR3i had travelled about 60 feet, the cop killer dropped down a gear and floored the accelerator. He overtook the XR3i and powered on down the road.

He had only just managed to put his gloves on when he saw the headlights of a car come up the road. He parked his motor a discreet distance. It should only take a few minutes to finish this job. He climbed out and waited quietly by the side of the house. As the Ford pulled into the small drive in front of the house, he pushed himself flat against the cold, damp brickwork of the semi. The Escort's lights went out and the cop killer fell to his hands and knees, quickly scrambling low along one side of the car, and waited at the rear of the vehicle. He looked back at the road but saw no one about. He heard the radio in the XR3i being switched off and as his head peered round the edge of the rear tyre, he saw the driver's door open and some black trousers and shoes step onto the wet ground. The Sergeant locked the door and turned to walk to the house.

The cop killer made his move like a snake with its tail rattled. His hand reached under his trouser leg and pulled out the knife strapped to his calf in a sheath.

Before the Sergeant heard anything, the black gloved hand was over his mouth and the knife slashed his throat. Blood gushed from the open wound as a scream died in the officer's throat. Just as he had read it in the 'Black Medicine' handbook, the cop killer carried out the killing manoeuvre with expert precision. The Sergeant struggled only briefly but Lloyd held a firm grip on his mouth. With his other hand he plunged the knife into the Sergeant's chest. Blood continued pumping from the neck wound and within a minute the police officer lay dead. The cop killer wiped the blade of the knife on the Sergeant's trousers, then searched for his wallet. He also took the officer's watch.

The operation had been silent, quick, ruthless and brutally effective. The cop killer looked carefully out of the drive at one end of the street, then the other. The coast was clear. Briefly he turned to look at the crumpled body of the Sergeant lying in a large pool of his own blood. The cop killer had no feelings for the man and was only concerned, as he climbed into the Sierra, to get the fuck away from there.

TEN

Dear Jackie,
I write to keep you informed about my work. No doubt by the time you get this letter you will have heard about the death of Sergeant Keith Summers. Fuck him! I saw on the news this morning that the police believe the motive for his murder was robbery. I just can't believe how stupid those cops are. The reporter asked the cop if there was any link with the Stockwell attack. The cop said there was no evidence to link the two. Either they are dumb as hell or I am very lucky. I wonder if God is looking out for me. Who knows, he may understand what I have to do.

I know sooner or later my luck will run dry, but for the moment why should I give a fuck? They're not even looking for me so I can continue shooting up every cop in sight instead of ducking and diving. By the time I'm through, they'll wish they never came across me, 'cause I'm not an amateur and I've got more reasons than a regular cop killer. I'll shoot one in a minute and think nothing of it. And that's something they'll have to learn. When they come for me eventually they'd better be prepared for a bloodbath of dead officers. And when they see my potential for badness and feel what it's like to be hunted down, they'll fear me and maybe then I'll get my point across: that they need to learn to treat us with respect, 'cause we can use guns too.

Jackie, I know you can write with feeling and perception. When I finally have to take what's coming I would like people to know why I did what I did. That is why it's important that I write these letters to you, so that soon you will be able to tell the community why I did it.

I read in The Inquirer the story about the death of Michael

129

Watts in Hackney. It was unfortunate that you chose to report exactly what the filth told you. For the record, his killing was not drugs-related in the usual sense. I killed Michael Watts because he was a parasite, a harbinger of death. He dealt in misery for our community so I had to let him know who he was fucking with. Street justice. His end was fitting justice. The Bible says to "stop the wickedness of evil men and reward those that are good." Michael Watts got his just deserts. So did Summers, so too will all the other oppressors and destroyers.

The end of my work is not too far away now but there are still things I must do. I have sent you some proof that what I say is the truth. Keep the faith.

The Cop Killer.

At that moment Jackie felt a rush of excitement come over her. She wanted to shout and tell the whole office that she had finally got the big story but she couldn't; this was too important to do that. This was a story too huge even for The Inquirer. No, this was her meal ticket to a forty grand job in the first division. If she could get this right she could negotiate a job on a national, no problem.

Jackie Spencer pushed the letter back into the padded envelope and made her way to the ladies. With the door locked she was able to examine more closely the other contents of the envelope without attracting the attention of her colleagues. She reached into the packet, pulled out a bullet and looked at the stamped markings at the base of the cartridge. .45 ACP S&W. She also found Sergeant Summer's blood-stained driving licence.

She sat down on the toilet seat and caught her breath. This was serious stuff, she thought. She pondered all the possibilities. Was she committing an offense by withholding this information from the police? She thought long and hard about the matter. For fifteen minutes she sat there, going through every permutation in her mind. Which ever way she looked at it she was taking a big risk with her career and with the law by keeping this letter a secret. But what were the alternatives? To carry on writing about people who had damp council flats in Lambeth and wanted a transfer? This was her one big break that had simply fallen in her lap, she couldn't just kiss it goodbye. If she played things carefully, she reasoned, she could minimise the risks to herself. Who, after all, knew she had received this letter?

She decided to wait and see what more correspondence came from the cop killer and try and get as much information as possible on this man. She left the toilet and returned to her desk.

"I was just about to send out a search party for you," her colleague said. Jackie smiled, trying her best to act normal.

"Oh Janice, I never knew you cared so much. I missed you too!"

With her colleague engaged in a telephone conversation, Jackie took the opportunity to check out a detail with a contact at Scotland Yard.

"Martin, you've been really helpful thanks for the information." Jackie put the phone down with a slight smile on her face. The police contact had confirmed what calibre weapon had killed Michael Watts. "A .45 automatic, probably a Colt pistol," he had said. She felt good. Everything was starting to fall into place...

The black Jaguar saloon car slowly turned off the main road and through the open iron gates. An army of photographers and TV cameramen, standing on the pavement by the gates entrance, surged forward to take photographs of the important-looking man in uniform in the back. An old woman watching the proceedings was told by a young photographer that the man was the

Metropolitan Police Commissioner.

"Oh that's a nice uniform he's got, innit Elsie? Very smart," the old woman turned to her friend who stood gawping at the steady stream of important looking cars and passengers pouring in through the gates of Nunhead Cemetery.

There were so many police officers in attendance that it was difficult to tell who was there to pay their last respects and who was there on duty. The black funeral cars were led by a contingent of police officers. Sergeant Summers was going out in style. He had lived his life as a bent copper; now in death he was being buried as a hero.

The cop killer watched from the ranks of the media, taking in the atmosphere of the occasion. As the last car went through the gates, the hack pack moved *en masse* into the cemetery. Several hundred yards inside, a large group of people stood around the roped-off place of burial.

A rambling, gothic-style cemetery dating from Victorian times—the place felt like the setting for a horror film, with the looming grey sky adding to the supernatural feel of the occasion. The atmosphere felt dark, almost sinister. The cop killer scanned the rows of faces standing near the hole cut into the ground. Some of them couldn't hide the fear from their eyes. If Summers could be cut down so swiftly and effectively by a common mugger, it could happen to any one of them. The streets really weren't safe anymore. The woman sobbing into a handkerchief, while two young boys held her side, focused his attention. She was the grieving widow, he guessed. He understood her sorrow; he knew, he had suffered too. In any war there are many casualties, he thought, and by the time I'm done there will be many more funerals. He had no fight with the wives and children, but he would not let their suffering stop his war. He was on the side of right and justice. Jah was with him and he could not stop until the beast had been vanquished. He would thrust a sword through the heart of the beast, just as he had with the Sergeant and he could not be swayed from his goal.

The sunny afternoon in September, when his mother was buried, seemed so far away from this cold, damp day in winter. When he closed his eyes, Lloyd could still hear the soothing singing of the ladies from his mother's church. Six voices in harmony making every word of the song tear at his heart and sink into his soul. Like two soundtracks running at the same time in his head, he heard the singing and the pastor's voice from that September day, intercut with the fainter distant words of the vicar who was laying to rest the body of the Sergeant.

"Excuse me, have you got the time?"

He could not quite place the accent, but the voice was soft and polite. He opened his eyes and looked at the woman.

"Sorry, do you know what the time is?" she repeated.

The cop killer looked at the dead Sergeant's watch on his wrist.

"Oh, twenty five past three."

She smiled.

"Thanks... nice watch."

"Yeah. A dear friend gave it to me as a leaving present."

She was very smartly dressed and apart from him, she was the only other black face at the funeral. He was curious as to why the sister was there and she was curious as to why he was there.

"Where did your friend go?" She was still smiling.

The cop killer didn't understand the question. Somewhere amidst the gathered forces of law and order, a man was weeping.

"You said a friend gave you that watch as a leaving present."

133

"Oh yeah. I don't know. 'They seek him here, they seek him there, is he in heaven or is he in hell, that damned, elusive Pimpernel'."

She thought his humour slightly odd but smiled all the same.

"So who do you work for? I don't think I've seen your face on the circuit."

He sussed out now, what she did from her question.

"Oh nah, I'm not one of this lot." He pointed with his thumb at the pack of journalists standing nearby. "I came to pay my last respecks. What's your excuse?"

"I work for The Inquirer newspaper as a reporter."

Her answer took the cop killer by surprise and he was lost for words. He wanted to ask her name, but no that would just be too much of a coincidence, he thought. The surprise and confusion showed on his face.

"Okay, you're now going to tell me what's wrong with The Inquirer. Don't worry I'm used to it. Go ahead, feel free to criticise."

"No, I like the Inquirer, get it every week."

"Sorry, I misread your surprise. I thought like every other black person you were going to tell me off for working for such a tabloid paper."

"Not me. By the way, the name's Francis."

"Jackie, nice to meet you." She offered her hand.

"Listen Francis, looking at your rather nice watch, I had better be getting back to the office..... Bye." She had walked about fifty yards before the cop killer caught up with her.

"Listen, if you've got five minutes I'd like to walk with you. It's not every day you meet Jackie Spencer."

She smiled, clearly flattered that he knew her name and intrigued as to how he did.

"Hey, how do you know my name?"

"I told you Jackie, I'm a big fan of The Inquirer, and I'm a big fan of your writing. Listen, I know you're in a hurry but if you could spare five minutes I would really appreciate it. I'm trying to do some freelance writing but I don't know how to go about it. Any advice you might have would be appreciated."

Once again she was flattered that someone would want to seek out her opinion, and agreed to go for a quick drink. She suggested a winebar near Camberwell. He followed in his Sierra to the trendy Gallery Winebar on Denmark Hill. Inside they ordered two glasses of house white.

"Here's to you Jackie," the cop killer proposed, holding up his wine glass.

"Jackie, it's really good of you to give up your time like this. I can't believe I just met you like so. It's incredible."

"Francis, it's a pleasure. If I can be of help you're more than welcome. So, tell me what you're doing at the moment, and what sort of things you want to write about?"

He played with his wine glass and felt ill at ease with the question.

"Well I'm trying to get a few business things off the ground at the moment. I'm just sort of developing the plans and such like. I don't really like to say too much about them in case they don't really happen. You know what I mean? I would also really like to try and do some writing."

He could see from the look on her face that she didn't take what he was saying very seriously.

"I can see you think I'm talking rubbish Jackie. As you can probably guess, I haven't been to university and I'm just a regular guy, but I'm willing to give anything a go. Do you think I need to have a degree to be a writer?"

It was the reporter's turn to feel awkward. She was amazed that he was perceptive enough to read her mind. There were very few people who were able to see behind her carefully constructed facade. She was too polite to admit he was right, so she lied.

"Oh no Francis, you've got totally the wrong impression. I wasn't thinking that at all. At the Inquirer the reporters come from all different backgrounds. There are some with degrees and a lot that don't have them. I don't think that is important for being a journalist. You didn't say what sorts of things you want to write about?"

"I want to be an investigative reporter, writing features of importance to the black community..."

Jackie listened to him thoughtfully. She and so many of her colleagues had entered journalism with the same ideals, but within a year of being at The Inquirer each of them had become desperate to get to the glamour journalism of the nationals and television by any means necessary. And no one at The Inquirer was more desperate to make the move than Jackie Spencer.

"Do go on," she said sweetly, "which features specifically are you thinking about?"

"Well, I want to write about what I see going on. I want to expose the enemies in our midst. I think there are two enemies facing the black community: the enemies outside and the enemies within. For example, I want to write about the police and the drugs epidemic in our community. Drugs and police seen from a black perspective are two agents sent to try and destroy us. I think..."

She cut him.

"Hold on there. I think it's very dodgy to try and make generalisations about any organisation, group or people. To try and say the police are all alike is rubbish."

The debate carried on backwards and forwards for some time. While he was polite and good natured in his arguments, there was something about the strength of hi belief that attracted her. He obviously believed strongly in his convictions and seemed prepared to suffer for them and though she normally sussed a person out within minutes of meeting them, this guy was very different.

The combination of the wine and the interesting debate made her lose track of time. When she asked him the time, it was five o'clock.

"Oh shit. I don't think I'll bother going back to work this late."

"I'm sorry Jackie, I've kept you."

She felt flustered and annoyed that she had lost track of time, but resolved not to let it bother her.

"Francis, don't worry about it. Let me buy you a drink. Same again?"

"Yeah. Safe."

She returned with the drinks and handed him a glass. The small wine bar was starting to get busier, as young professionals on their way home stopped off for a quick drink. An old converted shop, The Gallery still had the big, glass front window of it's previous life but it had been painted in parts with Art-Nouveau style images of flowers. Stripped pine tables, adorned with vases of fresh flowers and candles in wine bottles, gave the place a pleasant and cosy feel.

"Jackie, let me put a question to you. Do you think it wrong to take human life for a cause you believe in?"

"No I don't, but it all depends on what the cause is. The question is a bit too abstract for me to give a definite yes or no. It would depend on what the cause were and who the victims were."

The cop killer smiled and nodded his head. There was something about this guy she couldn't quite work out. But she wanted to get to know him more, another time maybe..

At eight o'clock she said she would have to be going. They walked to the door and shook hands.

"Jackie, it's been nice meeting and reasoning with you. Tek care. Respect."

"I've had a really interesting afternoon. If you need

any more help or information, you've got my card, so just give me a ring."

They said their goodbyes and headed off in different directions. The cop killer didn't feel much like working but he had told Sanjay he would be there for 9:00pm...

Lloyd put the key in the front door and went into his flat. It was nearly 9:00pm. In the kitchen he hurriedly put the bomb into a plastic bag and rushed back to the car. He would be on time to start work so he wasn't worried. How he would do what else he had to do, he wasn't sure. Runnings were going to be tight this evening, he thought.

ELEVEN

You are totally out of your mind. How could you think of doing such a stupid thing? I just don't believe you."

There was a look of fury in his face and he was fighting to remain in control of his rage. He paced up and down the lounge, toying with ornaments and other objects around the room. He would take a few paces, fiddle with something, then move to another part of the room to do the same. Jackie Spencer sat in a leather armchair shaking her head in disbelief.

"Ainsley, I regret telling you now. If I'd known this was the way you were gonna carry on, I 'd have kept my mouth well shut. I was telling you to get some advice, not to have you insult me, thank you."

It was her turn to get angry and her boyfriend could hear it in her voice. He decided to try and cool things down and stopped ranting. He sat down on the sofa and took a long, loud exaggerated sigh.

"Look Jackie, I'm only trying to make sure you don't get yourself into trouble. It's madness to walk around with this dead policeman's driving licence and a bullet from his murderer. You could get done for withholding vital evidence, or worse, they could try and say you were involved with the murder. Then they'll say the boyfriend had something to do with it. That's how they fit people up. Cho' man, ask the Guildford Four or the Birmingham Six how things stay. You think I'm going over the top just go and check them. Jackie, you know how things go."

She tired of his ranting.

"All I know is that this is my big break for a story. If I

do things your sensible and safe way I'll still be at the Inquirer in five years time. My career is everything to me so I'll take the risk. This is my chance to get on a national."

"Oh thanks very much Jackie. Now I know that I come second in your life to your bloody career...!"

News At Ten was just starting and the chimes of Big Ben were proving a distraction for Ainsley. He turned the sound down on the remote.

"...I just hope you've thought it through, because you might end up in prison, instead of in a better job..."

While all the other cars slowed down sharply for the upcoming police road side camera, the Sierra kept up it's 50mph speed. The two youngsters in the back looked at each other and smiled. The car turned sharply to the left off the Holloway Road and headed in the direction of Camden.

"You got tha' time, mate?" said the one with long, dirty-looking hair. He looked around eighteen, scruffy and the sort who liked to remove other people's car radios without asking.

"Just gone ten," came Lloyd's reply.

The cop killer had heard them talking about going to a club in Camden High Street, but they had told him to drop them at some nearby flats.

"You're listening to Ruffneck FM and the time has just gone ten minutes past the ten. I'm DJ Althea, riding the rhythms until the witche's hour, midnight, so hold tight and don't bother go nowhere. We're having a serious discussion right now about black men: are they an endangered species? Those are not my words but the sister from Edmonton who says 'the men must put dem house in order'..."

Lloyd couldn't hear too clearly what the youth was

140

saying so he turned down the radio.

"I said the turning's coming up on the right."

Lloyd nodded...

Ainsley had just entered from the kitchen with a beer in his hand. He sat down again and pulled the ring. He took a sip and thought about what he was going to say next. Jackie was sitting clutching a cushion round her stomach, watching the news.

"Jackie, I'm sorry I shouted at you. But I'm really concerned that this could get you into hot water. I think you should speak to your Editor, then get in touch with the police."

She sat quietly, still watching the television. When it seemed as though she was going to ignore Ainsley she said, "Thank you for your concern, okay I'll speak to my Editor." She was lying, but she didn't entirely trust Ainsley not to mess things up and it was better to leave him thinking she was going through the appropriate channels...

The Sierra pulled into the wide court at the front of the flats. As he glanced in his rear-view mirror he saw the long-haired youth whisper conspiratorially to his mate. He stopped the car at the requested spot and turned round to sort out the money.

"That's eight pounds please."

"To tell ya the truth, mate, we ain't gonna pay."

The youth had an insolent grin on his face and waved the small knife in his right hand threateningly before the cop killer's eyes. Lloyd saw the hand of the other guy reaching for the door handle.

"Can I make a suggestion?" Before the youngster had time to answer, Lloyd continued. "If you want to leave

141

wid yuh raas in one piece, I would fuckin' hand over eight pounds right now... A tip is left to the discretion of the customer." His voice was calm but purposeful.

The youth thought it was a bluff and made his move.

"Fuck off nigga!" His hand reached for the door handle.

The thud and scream came close together. Instant reaction. The force with which the butt of the cop killer's gun smacked the youth squarely on the nose was always going to break it with a crunch. The knife fell from the youth's right hand onto the floor of the Sierra, as his hand instinctively moved to stem the torrent of blood gushing from his nose. He wailed like a dying man as he fell out of the rear door onto the concrete yard. His mate had already light-footed it away like a frightened rabbit. The cop killer stepped out of the car and moved to the youth sitting on the ground holding his nose.

'That's eight pounds, please," he said calmly to the youngster.

The request made the kid bawl even more. The cop killer only needed to take one more pace forward to silence the youth's blubber and he hurriedly produced a ten pound note from his denim jacket pocket and handed it over. The cop killer folded the note and tucked it into the rear right hand pocket of his jeans.

"Am I right in thinking that this includes a tip?"

The youngster moaned some more and nodded his head eagerly.

"Well the way I check it is that too many guys are too quick to raise their hand. Black men are under a lot of pressure and I understand that. But what they have got to realise is that the black woman is there to support them and that we know what they are going through. I would say to the men: don't take your anger and frustration out on us. We are for you, not against

142

you..."

"Well thank you for that, Donna from Bruce Grove... You're listening to Ruffneck FM, and I'm DJ Althea. Remember, love the life you live, and live the life you love. Pure spiritual vibes on Ruffneck FM. Keep the calls coming..."

He filled up with petrol and cleaned up the blood as best he could from the back seat with paper wipes. The garage had the usual assortment of late-night boy racers, filling up and fiddling with their souped-up XRs, RSs, and GTis. It was a crowd who all seemed to know eachother and there was a lot of good natured jousting between the drivers and passengers of different cars.

The East End banter was a background noise to the cop killer. His attention was focused on the police station across the road. Housed in a small, old-fashioned building, Bethnal Green Police station sat on the corner of the main road and a very narrow side street. At the back was a small yard packed with police cars.

It was still too early for the operation to begin, but he wanted to get a feel of the surroundings before he came back. He felt excited and wanted to get on with the task at hand. He looked at his watch; it read 10:45pm...

Jackie lay in bed staring up at the dark ceiling, a thousand thoughts running through her head. At the end of the flat she could hear the muted sound of the television and the occasional clatter of crockery and cutlery in the kitchen. She was thinking about all the things that Ainsley had said to her. Had she really become ruthless and ambitious? He'd said that she was allowing a murderer to walk free for her own selfish reasons. Now she wondered if he was right.

She turned to lay on her side and could see a faint reflection of her face in the ceramic lamp base, on the bedside table. A ray of light ran across the bed to the table from the slightly opened bedroom door. She thought about getting up to turn off the hall light, but couldn't be bothered. She thought about Francis and their conversation in the wine bar. He did seem a bit strange, but there was something she liked about about him. Maybe it was his almost child-like reasoning about things? There was no middle ground for him. He wasn't politically correct, but knew exactly what he believed in and there was no moving him from that. She admired his commitment. She wasn't sure exactly *what* he believed in, that bit wasn't too clear, but he seemed to be focused on whatever it was.

Was she even enjoying this job of hers or was she still trying to prove a point to her parents and the doubters back in Wales? She sometimes wondered. How was she going to get herself out of this situation without getting into trouble with the police?

What was she going to do about her relationship with Ainsley? Recently it had just become a series of rows and long periods of sulking afterwards. Did she really need this? Did she really want it? Were they right for each other...?

"A lot of times it's the women that cause the problems. I'm telling you. They demand this, they want that. They're totally out of order. I meet 'nuff woman who think some man's gonna come on a white horse and take them away from it all. That's foolishness, man. I think the average black man's got it a whole heap tougher than a woman. And I mean that. No, seriously, whereas the white man will give a black woman a job, he won't give the black man the job. I'm telling you. They're scared of the black man. It's the fear of the black dick. I'm telling you..."

"Basil from E8 there. Personally, I think the man ah chat a whole lot of do-do. But what do you think? You've got another

He tipped the last bits of sensi from the small plastic bag onto the tobacco. Carefully picking the seeds and stalks out he deposited them back into the bag and dropped it out of the window. He skillfully rolled the rizla and tobacco and licked the glued edge of the paper. He finished off with a roach, then lit up. It was his last bit of weed and he was going to savour it. He made a mental note to get down to Herbsman in Brixton tomorrow.

He was reading a copy of the Daily Mirror and his focus was on the story on page five: '£100,000 BOUNTY ON HEADS OF POLICE KILLERS'.

'Film director, Joseph Bramers, has put up a £100,000 reward to help catch the killers of two policemen.'

He finished reading the story then tossed the paper onto the passenger seat. He drew hard on the spliff while he contemplated his next move. It looked like the cops didn't have any specific leads to go on. The Summers killing was being treated as a vicious street robbery and in the Stockwell attack the two boys had still not been picked up by the police. He thought his time was running out and he reckoned on another two weeks or so to complete his task.

He leaned back, resting his head on the car seat's headrest and slowly inhaled the ganja. Outside on the pavement, the dregs from Bethnal Green's closing pubs stumbled past in noisy conversation.

In a sensi-induced dream his mind drifted off to a different time when he could hear the reggae music of a blues dance pumping in his head. The bass was echoing and some melodic horns were coming through from the backing track.

"Roots music, seems to be going around,

145

Roots music, seems to be top of the town,
Jah Jah, him love it, in country and all over town,
The dread, him ah scrub it, its rhythm won't let you down."

The words of the song were clear to him and he could feel the sweaty heat of the rammed dance on his face.

He was standing against the wall eyeing the girls and catching the vibes. He had just turned seventeen and dressed in a sharp silk jacket and pants and a brand new Kangol he felt he was a big man. He leaned against the wall of the community centre as the dance bubbled nicely, his head bobbing to the pulsating drum and bass, a can of Brew in one hand, a four-rizla spliff in the other. 'No man can test we,' he had thought at that moment in time and he really did believe it.

As that seventeen-year-old ghost put the spliff to his mouth, so too did Lloyd ten years on. The cop killer smiled as the memory came to him. It had all seemed so simple then.

As the spliff came to an end so did his memories. He flicked the roach out of the window and headed back towards Swift Cars...

He put his hand on her shoulder, but he could tell from her total lack of response that it was not going to be a night of lustful pleasures of the flesh. She was still moody, he thought because of his response to her behaviour, but she was anxious also about the decision she had made.

"Jackie, have you set the alarm?"

A grunt that sounded like "yes" came from the other side of the bed. She remained in the foetal position with her back to him.

"Jackie, how are you going to follow up the story? You can only do more if he writes more detailed letters to you, or, God forbid, tries to get in touch with you by som other means."

Jackie turned over to face him.

"I have a feeling that at some point he will get in touch. The guy is obviously a complete nutter and I think for some reason he wants to speak to me. I want the story but don't worry I wouldn't take any chances with my safety to get it."

Even as she said it, she knew that the statement was far from the truth...

The old man's hand was shaking as he passed the money to Lloyd.

"Sorry young man, old age catching up with me. Worst thing you can do is to get old. I don't recommend it."

The cop killer got out of the car to help the old man out. He supported him with one hand and reached into the car for pensioner's walking stick. The old man thanked him, then slowly shuffled off to his front door.

Plaistow wasn't the sort of place Lloyd wanted to grow old in. Its grimy, grey streets and houses seemed a sad backdrop for life's colourful stage. He looked at his watch, it was nearly midnight...

Since leaving Plaistow nearly two hours had passed, as he cruised around the streets of the capital, thinking and listening to music. Driving was a good way to free the mind. The constantly changing images of the city gave him a sense of freedom and escape. It didn't matter where you lived in London if you had wheels you could be anywhere. He passed the bright lights of Piccadilly Circus and drove along the Embankment, along the 'another world' streets of Chelsea and up towards Ladbroke

147

Grove. Northwards as far as Harlesden, then back towards Kilburn and Camden.

It was just him, the sounds, and the city streets. Along Kings Cross he gazed out at society's rejects and undesirables living out their lives: the pimps and drugs dealers, the haggard prostitutes touting for business, the tramps and the alcoholics. The old and the unwanted, the dirty and the unclean. It was a neon-lit world of broken dreams and wasted life.

"One day a real rain's gonna come and wash all the scum of the sidewalk," he said out loud to himself.

It was the line from a film whose title he'd long forgotten, but the dialogue stayed in his head. Now seemed the right moment to call the words from memory. Lloyd hated Kings Cross and really did wish that one day that rain would come, and one day soon.

It was 2:00am. Time he went to work. He steered his motor in the direction of Bethnal Green, but took it easy. The last thing he needed right now was a pull from the radics.

He turned left by the police station and drove down Corfield Street. He parked at the bottom of the road and checked no one was about before taking the plastic bag out of the car boot. He walked up Corfield Street, praying that no cops were going to appear on the scene. As he turned the corner he could see the open gates to the small yard at the back. At the back of the station was a portacabin-type building, which was obviously linked to the main building by a door. The lightweight hut was supported on a metal frame, which in turn sat on the concrete of the yard. A light was on in the portacabin and although the glass windows were of a frosted finish he could she people moving inside the building.

He knew the rough layout of the yard, having driven down this small side street before, but he had not thought where he would plant his bomb. He knew he would have to decide quickly.

As he approached the yard he crossed over the road to be on the same side as the entrance. He hoped no police car would turn the corner at that point and that no one would walk out of the back door of the station that led into the yard. He stopped, looked into the yard, then darted to the back of two parked patrol cars. He scanned quickly around the yard, deciding on his play. He was about to move when the back door of the station flew open. He ducked back behind the squad car and could hear the the two officers in conversation about a football match. The voices got louder and he realised that they were walking towards the vehicle. Then he heard the door of the station open again and more voices come into the yard.

He knew exactly what was happening. The cops were going out on patrol in the two cars he had chosen to hide behind. If they pulled off he would be left exposed in the yard. He needed to move out quickly to the back of the other car parked nearby. However, if he broke cover there was a real possibility that, even in the dimly lit yard, he would be spotted. He looked around and found a large stone by his shoe. It was a risk but he was a man with only one ace up his sleeve.

He lobbed the stone over the yard wall into the side street. It landed with a sharp crack on the pavement. The cops looked at each other, then in the direction of the entrance. With their backs turned towards him, it was his only chance. He crouched low and quietly darted from behind the car's rear to the back of the other car parked about twelve feet away. After investigating and finding nothing in the street, a cop joined his colleagues and they drove out of the yard in the two vehicles.

He crossed the yard quickly and crawled underneath the portacabin. The metal frame legs supporting the cabin were less than two feet high, so space underneath the cabin was tight. He shuffled along on his back, like a mechanic underneath the belly of a large vehicle.

In the office overhead he could hear the mumbled voices of the officers and see the floor of the building flex as the occupants moved about. His eyes scanned the underside, looking for a suitable site for the bomb. A metal support running across the width of the building was chosen. Removing the pipe bomb from its polythene holder, he secured it to the metal girder with a length of wire he had included in the bag. With his cigarette lighter he put the flame to the fuse.

Now was the riskiest part of his mission. He scurried out of the belly of the beast and ran across the yard and into the street. Once again Lady Luck was shining down on him. There were no police cars driving into the yard to catch him red-handed. He had tested various lengths of fuse in his flat, timing the burning speed of various sizes of oil lamp wick. He had calculated that he would have five minutes burning time.

Half-walking, half-running, the cop killer made his way down Corfield Street towards his car. He was just opening the door when he heard a loud 'boom' like the sound of thunder. The fuse had burnt too quickly. He started the car and pulled away, making sure to keep his lights off until he was safely around the corner. In Corfield Street, curtains moved, as sleepy flat dwellers peered out to discover the cause of their rude awakening.

The cop killer tried to keep calm and drive at a pace that would not attract police attention, but he had been shaken by the bomb going off prematurely. He was alot cooler when he was unsure if it was even going to work. Now he was wondering if the cops were already on his tail. He was doing about 40mph down the Whitechapel Road with only a mile to go through the dark streets when he noticed, in his rear view mirror, the lights of a car moving at speed behind him. He decided to get ghosted and indicated left at Stepney Green tube station. He wasn't looking for trouble. The car followed him and flashed its headlights. He pulled over and waited.

In his mirror he saw the one occupant of the unmarked Astra climb out of the car. The police officer put on his peaked cap and walked slowly towards the driver's door. The cop killer wound down the window and waited.

"Oh sorry mate, it's just routine. There's been a suspected IRA incident in Bethnal Green. Can I ask you to step out of the vehicle and open the boot please. I'll just have to do a check on your registration. It's the usual..."

Lloyd didn't give him the chance to finish the sentence. What happened next was the flex of a veteran. The officer had never seen anyone move so fast and it was going to be the last move he'd see in his life. Suddenly he was looking down the barrel of a .45 automatic in the black man's hand. It flashed through the cop's mind in that instant that he would die and he thought of the young wife he was leaving behind. This was something that rarely happened to cops and when it did, he never dreamt it could happen to him. Frozen with fear, he watched in slow motion as the gun was pushed into his face and fired at point blank range.

He never heard the sound of the gun, but was lifted off his feet by the bullet crashing into his face. He never felt the other bullets that hit him either. The first one had taken his life.

The street erupted with the sound of gunfire as shots licked from the automatic in the cop killer's hand. The .45 blasted three rapid fire shots into the officer's chest as he fell backwards onto the road... Shot after shot found its mark with deadly accuracy.

The cop killer stared down briefly at the motionless body of the cop sprawled out on the street. His rep had just got bigger. He put the car in gear and sped off.

He hadn't wanted a confrontation. Things had not gone to plan and he was cursing himself for messing up with the bomb. He gave up trying to drive at a sensible speed and blasted his way down the side roads towards Bow. He had to get back to the fort fast to find sanctuary.

Once inside the flat he set to work searching for any clues that could implicate him in the police attacks. He trashed the remaining piece of copper pipe from which he'd fashioned his home-made bomb, into a bin bag with the weed killer, then quickly loaded his pistol with more bullets and dumped the remainder into the bin bag. He collected up all the clothing he had worn in his operations and dumped them also. Three bin bags later, he was wondering whether to trash the gold rings on his finger.

He scrubbed the bathroom for hours, bleaching every nook and cranny where there may have been spots of blood or pieces of hair and fibre. Then it was the turn of the kitchen. Everywhere he looked there was some potential trap, some possible clue for the police. He started by cleaning one surface then another. The more he looked the more tiny crevices he could see which could trap him. He rolled up the carpet in the lounge and put it to one side for disposal; more than likely incriminating evidence had followed him into the flat under the soles of his shoes. But what about the sofa? The table? Did they harbour clues? And what about his record collection? All it took was a microscopic piece of forensic evidence. Like a man possessed, he went to work stripping his flat of nearly every movable item and scrubbing every inch of wall and floor space as if cleansing his soul of evil.

By the time the rising of the sun and the soreness of his hands stopped him from completing his task, only his bedroom remained untouched. He had slept on the sofa for so long now that he couldn't remember the last time he used the bed. Exhausted, he lay down on his bed and fell into a deep sleep.

TWELVE

Three office-type chairs were placed in precise positions behind the long, light-coloured table. In front of each chair on the table was a neatly arranged pad of paper and a couple of pens. Spotlights gave extra illumination to the table, which was positioned on a slightly raised platform. A screen covered in a grey tweed-type material provided a backdrop to the table and chairs.

The murmured chattering of the fifty or so people seated in rows facing the table stopped as the three police officers walked into the room and took their places on the platform.

The youngest of the three officers spoke first and introduced himself and the two other men present.

"Ladies and gentlemen, thank you for coming along to this Scotland Yard press conference. This morning at approximately 2:12 am there was a bomb explosion at Bethnal Green police station which caused serious injury to the legs of one officer and damage to a portable lightweight building at the rear of the station. The officer lost both legs as a result of the blast."

"Ten minutes later, an officer on patrol was shot and killed near Stepney Green. We are investigating whether these attacks are linked. And we are to investigate any possible links between these two incidents and the recent murders of two other police officers."

The officer went on to detail the injuries of the policeman who had been standing closest to where the bomb was planted. The officer then introduced the Metropolitan Police Commissioner, who talked of the danger that the force faced every day patrolling the streets of the capital.

Jackie Spencer sat in the second row from the front making copious notes and feeling extremely nervous. The seriousness and the growing scale of the affair was beyond anything she bargained for. She wondered how the officers present would react if they knew that one of the reporters at this press conference had vital evidence connected with the case.

After the three officers had made their points the journalists got to work with their questions. The likelihood of it being an IRA attack was not great, said one of the officers, because the bomb was of such a "crude homemade construction." Once the IRA connection was refuted the journalists were keen to develop the idea of a cop serial killer and the questions came thick and fast on this angle.

The younger cop said that at that moment there was not firm forensic evidence that linked the four separate attacks. After half an hour the conference broke up and the journalists started milling out of the double doors at the back of the room.

Jackie remained for a moment in her seat, putting her notebook back into her bag and wondering what her next move should be. She had heard about the midday press conference at New Scotland Yard when she got into work. She had told the Editor she was taking an early lunch, then rushed up to Victoria.

"Hello. I didn't think this one fell within the scope of the Inquirer." It was the voice of Trevor Greene —one of the few black crime reporters on a national newspaper. He was acquainted with Jackie through various black media events they had attended.

"Oh hiya. Long time no see. How's it going?"

As they made their way out of the conference room and towards the lift they chatted about the world of

154

journalism and aspects of the press conference.

Jackie said her only interest in the conference and the case was because the chief suspects in the Stockwell case were two black youngsters. As they went through the glass doors and into the cold, Trevor drew closer to her.

"Let me give you some strictly off the record and definitely not for publication info."

"A good contact of mine is involved in the case. He says that the police have some evidence that they are not releasing. They have witnesses from the attacks in Bethnal Green and Stepney Green who say they saw a black man in a blue Ford Sierra at both places. The police aren't going to release the information for fear of alerting him."

"They reckon that the guy probably lives in east London because he knew the layout of the station. They reckon it's someone who has a personal grudge against the station or police in general."

"They are mounting a big operation to check all the black owners of blue Ford Sierras within a six mile radius. They're keeping that quiet for fear of being called racist and alerting the guy."

Jackie thanked him for the information and headed towards the underground station...

Apart from the occasional angler sitting in hope, the banks of the Grand Union Canal were empty and lonely. A slightly foggy, grey, overcast day provided the cop killer with the perfect conditions for disposing of evidence. He strolled along the canal near Hackney Marshes, waiting until he reached seclusion underneath a bridge. Checking no one was about, he threw the piece of copper tube into the dirty waters. A handful of bullets followed, then the can of weedkiller. He had stopped off in Hackney on his return journey from Leyton where at the council tip, he dumped his lounge carpet, various items of clothing and the table from his lounge. Tomorrow he planned to have the few other remaining items thrown away and replacements bought.

The voice sounded familiar but she couldn't place it. She put her hand over her left ear so she could hear better in the din of the office.

"Sorry, I didn't hear all of what you said."

"Jackie, I think it would be useful if we could meet up today. There's a lot of things I need to discuss with you."

"Who am I speaking to please?"

"I have been in correspondence with you. You know me as the cop killer."

She was surprised but not shocked. It was more like a feeling of intense excitement. She knew that at some point he would try and get in touch. She wanted to ask a thousand questions but played it cool so as not to frighten him away or let the whole of the Inquirer editorial know what she was doing.

"I'm glad you got in touch, there's so many questions I'd like to ask you. When can we meet?"

"Okay that's cool. Listen, meet me tonight at 7:00pm at McDonald's in Brixton. I'll be wearing a green Miami Dolphins baseball hat... And please, Jackie, no funny business. I don't want to see any police or photographers about. You understand?"

She reassured him that she would come alone. When she put the phone down her hand was shaking. She imagined it was the feeling a shoplifter got as they walked out of the store, not knowing if they were going to get away with it or if they would feel an arresting hand on their shoulder. She wondered if it would end in glory or disaster. She also wondered if she really wanted to be going down this road. Since her argument the other night with Ainsley she had questioned her desire to become just another soulless, ruthless hack who would sell her mother to get the story. It was too late for moral dilemmas however, she was consumed by ambition and had made up her mind.

The afternoon work seemed to drag on. Her thoughts were totally on how she would deal with the evenings proceedings. She phoned the flat and left a message on the answerphone saying she was out on a story and would be home late. It was easier than phoning Ainsley at work and getting herself into more grief. The last thing she needed was a boyfriend on her case.

In a newspaper office tempers were often left with the safety catch off. Judging by the shouts of indignation coming from the Editor's office, someone's fuse was obviously burning down. Although it was a glass-walled room, rows of often closed blinds prevented clear visibility into the Editor's office. For the first time in the day a hush came over the newsroom as journalists tried to hear what was being said. Jackie scanned the room to see who was missing from their desk and had a booming voice. She reckoned it was the sports Editor, Winston Reeves.

"Bloodclaat!"

It was loud enough for the whole office to hear. From the sounds of crashing furniture there was clearly some sort of scuffle going on in the office.

"I'm gonna fucking take you apart!!"

"Jus' cool down, nuh!"

"I'll fucking cool you down!!"

"You're fired so why yuh nah jus' go?"

The scuffling carried on for a few more minutes until the sports editor stormed out of the office, cleared his desk, and disappeared out of the newsroom.

The incident provided the office with speculation and gossip for the rest of the afternoon and hurried along the passage of time. At 6:00pm most of the journalists started to go home for the day. Jackie used the relative quiet of the place to catch up on some of her news stories. At 6:50 she started to make her way to the McDonald's on the corner of Brixton Road and Acre Lane.

She turned up the collar of her coat as protection against the unusually chilly November evening. On the short stroll over to the fast food restaurant she thought about how she would play it with the killer. Car horns blared as one irate motorist cussed another for blocking the road. The icy wind hadn't stopped the usual crowd of men from gathering outside the Pacific pub. It was a Brixton way of life to hang out on street corners and Jackie mused that when she got her job on the nationals she would miss this long time tradition which even the cold weather couldn't halt. From early morning until late at night the streets of Brixton bustled with life. The good, the bad and the ugly and every other form of human life assembled there, like some kind of frontier town.

She could just make out the sign for the fast food restaurant now. Her heart began to pound heavily. She suddenly realised how nervous she was. What was she doing? Was she really arriving at a rendezvous with the most wanted man in Britain? For the first time, Jackie Spencer considered seriously her boyfriend's warning that the man could be dangerous.

She pushed open the glass door of of the restaurant and scanned around the. She heard a voice a fraction of a second before seeing the face.

"Jackie."

Oh no! Of all the times to bump into someone you know, she thought. She could hardly ignore the man but supposing the killer arrived while she was speaking to him? He would think that he was being set up, especially after she had told the killer that she would come alone. She would have to make the conversation ultra short.

"Hello Francis. What a nice surprise. How is the

freelancing coming along?" she said, her eyes darting around the restaurant, looking for a man wearing a particular baseball cap. She wasn't even listening to his reply, but smiled and nodded reassuringly as he spoke.

"Good, good. Listen, maybe we could meet up for another drink sometime and have a chat? It's just that I'm meeting someone in here. It's a delicate council story I'm doing. I don't want to scare him off by being seen with someone else. I told him I'd come alone. My apologies."

She was about to disappear when 'Francis' cut in.

"He wasn't wearing a green Miami Dolphins hat was he?"

She was taken aback by the question.

"Why do you ask?"

"Just two minutes ago, a brother with a Dolphins cap was sitting jus' over there when two police come and take the guy out to a car. The man didn't struggle or nut'n."

She looked shocked; like her world had fallen in.

"Jackie, is everything alright? You look upset, man."

"Sit down, let me get you a coffee."

The reporter sat down. She couldn't believe it. It was within her grasp then she'd lost it. Why did it always happen like this?

The cop killer returned with the coffee and passed it to her. Slowly, she started to regain her composure.

"Shit! I just can't believe it. That could have been such a big story for me. What did this guy look like?"

The cop killer shrugged his shoulders.

"Well a kinda regular black man, you know. He looked like he had a lot of problems on his mind." Lloyd had a smirk on his face.

She was not amused.

"This isn't a joke. This was a really important meeting. I've just kissed goodbye to my one big break," she exhaled a sigh of frustration, then remembered herself. "Look, I'm sorry... I wasn't having a go at you."

"Listen Jackie, come finish your coffee. Let me take you for something a bit stronger."

Her plans lay in ruins so she had nothing to lose. She accepted his offer and they went to a pub a few hundred yards up the road. A smart, newly-opened pub, The Duke of Monmouth, was a relaxing place to pop into for an evening's drink. He bought a couple of brandies and they sat at a table near the fireplace.

"You looked really upset back there. You sure everything is okay?"

She knocked back her brandy in one.

"As they say, easy come easy go. You want another, Francis?"

She ordered two more double brandies. The conversation rolled on and on all evening. They discussed just about every subject under the sun. The number of drinks consumed grew steadily.

By 10:00 pm their body language was indicative of a couple who'd known each longer than they had. He had even caressed her leg with his hand and she had responded by giving a drunken giggle. She kept an eye on the time at first, then after two more brandies gave up caring.

The cop killer had paid Herbsman a visit before arranging to meet Jackie and now had an ounce of pungent smelling sensi in his jacket pocket. He desired to have this woman tonight and knew the herb would do the trick. Now that he had cleaned up at home it was safe to invite someone around without fear of exposing his true identity. He suggested that they went back to his yard to have a spliff. To Jackie the idea sounded fun, so she took him up on the offer. It had been a while since she had really let her hair down.

"All work and no play makes Jackie a dull girl," she said smiling sweetly at Lloyd. They finished off their drinks and headed for his car.

Brixton to Bow was an easy half hour journey, yet by the time they got there Jackie had fallen into an unsober slumber. The cop killer had to support her from the car up to his flat. He opened the front door and she awoke as he carried her over the threshold to his almost bare flat. He took her coat and suit jacket and hung them up in the cupboard in the hall.

"Excuse the state of things; I'm redecorating and getting new furniture. It might be better if we chilled out somewhere more comfortable."

"Oh yeah! I bet you say that to all the women... Oh come on then, lead the way."

They relaxed on the bed in his sparsely-furnished, shabby bedroom. She felt tired and laid on her back looking up at the ceiling. He started to build a spliff with a kingsize rizla. He had plenty of weed so he didn't bother adding tobacco.

The spliff felt strong and after a few pulls he began to feel charged. Jackie took a couple of puffs then lay her head on the pillow her thoughts a million miles away from Bow. The cop killer went next door and slipped an old-time lover's tape onto the hi-fi, before returning to the bedroom. The soulful reggae wafted through and the song of the female harmony trio told of finding 'the love of a lifetime'. Lloyd felt mellow. It didn't take a genius to suss out the way things were going to run. Everything was copasetic.

Jackie lay curled up on the bed, softly singing along to the record. Lloyd rested the spliff in the ashtray and lay down beside her. He kissed her gently on the lips and ran his tongue in and out of her mouth playfully, while slowly undoing the buttons of her black blouse. As he pulled open the silky fabric, the glimpse of her uplifted cleavage in the black lace bra, made him stiffen.

Nothing else mattered, but her body which cried out for his caressing hands. He admired the smooth, dark

161

skin of her bosom, transfixed as her breasts heaved with her sighs. He reached behind her back, unhooked her bra and lifted it up to reveal her firm rounded breasts. Gently, he rubbed her nipples and watched them stiffen to his touch then gently squeezed them between the tips of his thumb and forefinger, urging them to even greater firmness. He licked round them and the warmth of his mouth made her quiver with pleasure. As he did so his right hand worked its way under her skirt, rubbing the inside of her thigh. She was wearing stockings which gave his fingers easy access to her panties and what lay beyond their confines. He could feel her wetness soaking through the underwear, as he slowly rubbed the back of his hand over her.

When he had further aroused her, his middle and forefinger slipped their way round her lacy underwear and stroked the lips of her wet pussy, gently working his fingers into the moistness, as she gently rocked backwards and forwards. Her hip movements got steadily quicker and her moaning louder.

"Oh that's good," she murmured. "Take your clothes off and lets get into bed,"she purred.

Lloyd pulled off his sweat shirt and T-shirt, then started unzipping his jeans. Meanwhile, she began sliding out of her skirt.

She lay on the bed in her panties, stockings and suspenders and looked up at him giggling.

"You're a very rude boy, aren't you!"

Her Welsh accent was now more pronounced after alcohol and it made her voice sound soft and sensual.

He hungrily started to pull her panties down and she lifted her pert bottom off the bed to help him in his task. He took his time removing her underwear, so much to tease himself as her.

She looked him in the eye and gave him a mischievous wink. With her stocking-clad legs opened wide, he could see the lips of her wet pussy glisten in the dim light of the room. She teased him, laying wide her legs so he could get a brief view of her punnany, then closing them, cutting short his peep show. Again her legs would open and she would run a finger slowly along the inside of her thigh until it reached her pussy and then further teased him by sliding two fingers over her clitoris before slipping them into her pussy.

At first he tried to play it cool and ignored her teasing, but it was too much for his will-power. He opened her closed thighs with his hand and went to work. His tongue felt the warm wetness as it moved in and out of her like a small but creative penis. Her hands clutched the back of his head and she pulled him tighter towards her. The tip of his tongue darted again and again along her swollen clitoris, until she let out a loud, powerful moan as she reached orgasm.

It felt so good she wanted more. He slipped a rubber over his rock-hard penis. The thrill of bringing her to climax with his tongue had made his dick get even stiffer.

As he got closer she gripped his cock and guided it towards the entrance of her pussy.

"Ahhhhh!" She let out a moan of pleasure and pain, as his cock gradually worked its way inside her.

Lloyd had to take deep gulps of air to slow his beating heart and dizzy head.

He started slowly; pulling his cock back until the head was at the lips of her pussy. Then he would slide it in right up to the hilt. Gradually the swiftness of his motion increased, until he was grinding her like a man possessed.

The bed shook as he rode her. Their breathing became harsh, the sounds echoing in the empty flat. She cussed him, urging him to zoom her harder.

"Come on you bastard, fuck me harder! Come on, harder!" she goaded.

When he thought he could give no more, he felt a rush

in his head and a surge in his balls. The orgasm was like an electric shock hitting his body. With an abrupt scream she tried to slip from his hold, but he gripped her buttocks tightly as his body shivered. He reached his peak and his cock pumped its seed. Jackie's moans of joy changed to words of endearment as he slipped from her sweaty body and stretched out beside her...

He had no idea what the time was but he knew it wasn't all a dream. His dick hurt too much for even the most erotic of dreams. A grind was a grind and he could still tell the difference even though he felt drunk, doped-out and dizzy. There was something else though; the throbbing in the side of his face. He opened his eyes to see her dressed and standing by the side of the bed. He then realised that she had hit him on the side of his face.

"You fucking lying bastard, you! You fucking shit! You've fucking ruined everything for me. Oh Christ, what am I going to do?"

He didn't have time to ask her what she was talking about.

"I know who you are. You're the fucking cop killer aren't you Francis, or should I say Lloyd?"

He jumped out of bed, pulling on his jeans and sweatshirt. He was trying to get everything together in his head and figure things out. He rubbed his eyes and tried to think coherently.

"Jackie, what's going on?"

She threw a fist at his face but he stopped it and held her wrist, while trying to contain her anger. He was vexed now, and with a little twist of her wrist made sure she knew it.

"Don't bother with any more stunts like that." He spoke slowly and deliberately. She knew that he meant it.

"Fuck you!" she spat helplessly.

164

He finally released her and walked out to the lounge, sat down and put a cigarette in his mouth.

"Okay Jackie, wassup?!" he called out through the open bedroom doorway.

She walked into the lounge from the hallway and stood by the kitchen door.

"After you were sleeping I felt thirsty, so I went to get some water from the kitchen. I sat down in here and saw a book on the shelf that interested me. When I pulled it out to look at it I noticed all the newspaper cuttings hidden behind the books. After I read them I knew it had to be you."

"I looked in your wallet and saw the name on the driving license, then it was obvious —'Lloyd Baker'. Lots of cuttings about Verone Baker. Remember, I spent a lot of time on that story. I interviewed Phillip Baker. I presume you are Phillip's brother? Yeah?"

The cop killer nodded as he inhaled hard on his cigarette.

"You're a clever woman Jackie. A very clever woman." He blew out a long cloud of smoke then drew hard again. "Jackie I'm sorry about lying to you. I was just trying to cover my back. Yah know what I'm saying?"

She took a cigarette out of the packet on the sofa and lit it. She sighed.

"God, I must have been out of my fucking head! What made me come here and screw you? I must be mad, or pissed and spliffed out of my fucking brains! It's the end of my career. Can you imagine the headlines when it come out. 'JOURNALIST'S NIGHT OF PASSION WITH CRAZED COP KILLER'." She moved her hands, as though she was sticking down the headline of a newspaper. "How on earth am I going to explain this when it comes out?" She puffed on her cigarette while she thought about a solution. "Well I could always tell the truth and explain how I was tricked. Yeah, there's nothing

165

strange about that. Of course everyone will think I'm a right slack bitch and my boyfriend will leave me, but at least I'll have the story, eh?"

She was sarcastic, but underneath the tone she was angry and worried.

"Jackie, don't bother distressing yuhself. It done and it finish. No one's going to hear 'bout this evenin', not from me anyway. That goes for the radics and press too. Believe me."

She was quiet now, sitting hunched up on the sofa with her elbows resting on her knees. She was trying to make sense of it all. She couldn't believe she had slept with a man who was practically a stranger. How was she going to explain her night out to Ainsley? She'd had sex with a dangerous killer. Was she crazy? Why didn't she just leave when she discovered the truth? How could she have enjoyed sex so much with a total stranger? She kept asking herself the questions over and over in her mind. It was all so out of character. Was it the drink or the weed, or both? She never drank very much and hardly ever smoked sensi; maybe that was it? She started to compose and calm herself. What was done was done and there was no going back, but there was just a possibility that she could salvage something out of this fiasco, she considered. After a while she spoke.

"Lloyd, do you mind if we do an interview? I need to know how and why you killed those police officers?"

The sudden change in tact didn't surprise the cop killer. "Jackie, go right ahead. Ask me anyt'ing you want. "

The reporter went and got her handbag and took out a small tape recorder. She placed it on the arm of his chair and switched it on. She started off by asking him questions about who he had killed, how and when. Then she asked him why he had done it. She asked lots of questions and he answered them. She didn't understand everything he said about his reasons and the way he

166

viewed the world, but she could at least grasp why he turned from being an anonymous mini-cab driver to being a murderer. It all started when the police brutally killed his mother.

While the rest of the world viewed him as a sick killer he saw himself as someone who was fighting a justified war against corrupt oppressors. "There ain't no justice-just me!" he said repeatedly, and he really did believe it. He was on a self-obsessed *jihad* against the evil that had shattered his life and he was taking no prisoners. She was fascinated by the contradictions of his personality. One side was easy-going and pleasant, while the other was dark and disturbing; a man who could kill and not be concerned about it; a cause without constraints.

She lit another cigarette and turned the tape over.

"A lot of youts nowadays choose the rough way," he continued. "Robbing, stealing and so on. What kinda way is dat, enh? People say they're bad. But you need to ask why they are like that? T'ings rough out deh, yah know. An' in militant times you need a militant solution, seen? If those youts had opportunities they'd stand a chance, but they ain't got none..."

The cop killer got up and walked across to the window. He stared out across the dark halogen-lit expanse of concrete.

"Jackie, I don't know if it makes any sense. What I'm trying to say is there's a lot of fuckin' angry people out there, potential killers just waiting for a target; someone to take the anger out on. And everyday they're gettin' stress from the system. Then one day the police come and gun their mother down, how they gonna feel? How d'you expect me to feel? They've gotta pay for it, else I'm not my mamma's son. And they're gonna pay good. 'Cause I don't care if I get killed. If Mama was alive, I wouldn't do this shit. But she's not..."

Jackie stopped the tape and walked to the window.

Lloyd's anger terrified her. Even as he spoke his eyes burned with fire and righteous revenge. How far would he go to get his 'justice'? She could put an end to all the killing by simply picking up a phone, but that would plunge her in a dilemma over 'journalistic ethics'. She originally agreed to meet him in strict confidence. What was she to do now?

"Let's call it a day with the interview," she said with a sigh. "I've got enough material. What about building up another spliff? I could do with calming my nerves."

He went to the kitchen and made some coffee before returning to build the spliff. It was 4:30am. He passed her the lit spliff two minutes later and she took several long, strong pulls of the herb. She burst into a small fit of laughter soon after but didn't know why. The cop killer smiled and shook his head. The question was unexpected after the giggling:

"Have you got the gun here?"

"Why d'yah ask?"

"I'm just curious, I've never seen a real gun before."

"Yeah, no problem."

He fetched the gun from the bedroom, emptied the bullets from it, then passed it to her.

She gripped the heavy steel gun with both hands round the handle, pointed it at the wall and took aim.

"Pow...! Pow...! Fuck, this thing's heavy. I never knew they were so heavy. If Sony made this it would be about a quarter of the size and have headphones." She laughed at her own silliness. "So Lloyd, what's it like when you shoot someone with this thing?"

The cop killer wasn't sure if the question was inspired by the ganja or whether it was the way her nervous system was dealing with the situation. He smoked the spliff unhurriedly, chilling, then looked across and smiled at her without answering.

"Oh, I nearly forgot... Lloyd, I'm not sure if I should be

telling you this, but the police are checking out black guys who own blue Ford Sierras and live in the East End. You were seen by witnesses in Bethnal Green and Stepney... I got the information from a journalist friend."

Lloyd nodded, but didn't say anything. He thought about the information she'd just given him and wondered how this would affect his plans. Yeah, he needed to get rid of the car as soon as possible. It was still registered to the person he'd bought it from after answering an ad in Loot, so that wasn't a problem. They had no easy way of tracing it to him via a DVLC computer.

He turned and smiled at Jackie. It was a shame their relationship couldn't have much future because of his chosen path. She would have been his ideal woman.

THIRTEEN

He pushed the nozzle into the red plastic container and carefully pulled back the handle. The petrol foamed up inside the container as he slowly filled it. After securing the top, he dumped it in the boot of his car.

It was a cold December night and outside of the warmth of the car The cop killer regretted not putting on a jumper before stepping out of his yard. He clasped his hands to keep them warm as he made his way to the glass booth of the Holloway Road garage.

The petrol station attendant, who was looking at a sex magazine under the counter, was startled as the cop killer banged on the glass.

"Dat t'ing will make you go blind, boss."

The young Asian man dropped the magazine and smiled, embarrassed.

"Oh, and give me twenty B&H and two boxes of matches please."

He took his change and quickly walked back to the car. He jumped in and in his hurry dropped his keys on the floor of the car. While rummaging on the floor he heard what was said but didn't know what it meant.

"Cho'. If he don't move it just ram into it."

He looked up. Four black youths were pushing a tatty blue Datsun sports car in the direction of where he was parked. He could see that they wanted to pass down the aisle he was in and park the dead vehicle against a wall at the side of the garage. He looked again on the floor for the keys. The youths' car was now about fifty feet away.

"Cho'. Just move yah fuckin' car, man!"

The guy was about 20 years old; tall, of dark complexion and wearing a black leather baseball-style jacket with a few gold chains. His hair was cropped and he looked angry.

"You fucking deaf, man? I said move your car."

The cop killer got out of the car and walked over to the man. He was calm and polite.

"Listen man, I'm not deaf, I heard you clearly. I've lost my car keys and I'm looking for them, okay?"

He turned and started walking back to the car.

"If you don't move that car quick, I'll fucking move you and the car. Yah damn pussyclaat! Jus' move it!"

He heard the others laugh.

The car was stopped about twenty feet away as they waited for him to go. The tall youth leaned against the side of the vehicle nearest to the cop killer. His homeboys stood on the other side of the Datsun.

The cop killer found the keys and started up the car. As he pulled away he heard the shouts of the tall man.

"Yeah, that's it, fuck off yah bumbaclaat."

The others were laughing and jeering.

He stopped the Ford. In his rear-view mirror he watched them start pushing the Datsun again. The tall man was gripping the top of the car as he heaved it along, his back to the cop killer's Sierra.

The cop killer put the car into reverse and slowly started backing up. When he got to within twenty feet of the Datsun's side he floored the accelerator. He heard one of the youths shout a warning to his tall spar but it was too late. As he turned to look, the Sierra's rear bumper was inches away from his knees.

The car hit him with enough force to slam his back hard against the side of the Datsun, his elbow breaking as it was forced through the passenger door window. The impact shattered his knee caps and made a large dent in the car's passenger door.

His mates stood back in shock. The Asian attendant had his hands on the glass, his mouth wide open in disbelief. The cop killer drove forward fifteen feet and stopped. As he walked towards the man lying on the ground and screaming in agony, he shook his head.

"Star, when yuh deh inna yuh wheelchair, yuh mus' learn respeck, seen? Learn respeck, yout'man, an' come correc'."

The man seemed to bawl out more as he clutched his grotesquely mangled legs. The cop killer got back in the Sierra and headed north.

"We ah de biggest, baddest, boldest, de broadest. We ah de ruffest and de tuffest. Nah bother come check our size.... 'cause we ARE D-a-n-g-e-r-o-u-s."

"The jingle says it all. Ain't that the truth. You're locked in to Ruffneck FM, causing some serious ruckshuns on the airways tonight. London consider yuhself warned!"

The traffic along the North Circular Road was moving sweetly and he settled down to a comfortable 45mph cruising speed. What was the matter with these bad bwoys? Why did they have to disrespeck their fellow brother so? The cop killer was still vexed with the young upstart for bringing trouble down on his own head like that. In another time, Lloyd would have bitten his tongue and gone about his business. But enough was enough. He wasn't going to take the shit from anyone anymore. It seemed like the world was becoming a jungle where man would eat dog to survive. If that was the way they wanted it, that's the way he would deal the cards. He knew why they turned out bad, but he wasn't gonna be no rude bwoy's punch bag. As his father used to say: " Don't wake a sleeping dog unless you can stand the bite." Well this was one dog who wasn't going to roll over and play dumb anymore. If they wanted to come and fuck with him then they had better be able to take the licks, whether it was the cops, or scum like Michael Watts, they had all better watch out.

He took his anger out on the road and stomped the go pedal to the floor. The speedo needle moved up to 80 mph and the aging Ford started to rattle and roll down the three-lane black top. He shouted to no one in particular. His hands banging the steering wheel as if he were goading the car into a fight.

"Don't tes' me...! Don't tes' me...! Don't tes' me...!"

He shouted it over and over again, like it was a Ninja warrior chant.

The hardcore rap tape in the stereo was turned up full tilt and the window was wound right down to let the cold night air cool his head down. The road ahead was totally clear and as he sped down the North Circular, music pumping, he fired off a couple of rounds from the .45 auto. His left hand gripped the wheel, while his other hand pointed the gun skywards out of the window. The booming blasts of the big bore 'matic echoed in the chilling darkness of the night. He felt alive and buzzing.

As he roared down his highway to hell the cop killer remembered the words of his dying father. "Bettah to live a day as a lion, than a lifetime as a sheep." Yeah, his old man got it right there.

The traffic light ahead was on red. As he slowed down in the outside lane he saw there were no others cars about. He stopped and took aim at the red glass of the signal. The impact shattered the glass into a thousand pieces and the redness vanished. He didn't bother for the lights to change. He just dropped the clutch and smoked the tyres away from the lights...

The car's suspension crashed and jolted every time the car hit a hole in the rough ground. He had to keep the speed up at around 15 mph for fear of the tyres sinking in the mud if he travelled any slower. The car's headlights provided the only real illumination over the waste ground situated roughly three miles north of Wood Green, the nearest streets being hundreds of yards away.

He put his face close to the windscreen, so as to see the terrain more closely. The rough patch of weed-covered ground was littered with all types of discarded waste, both domestic and industrial. Large chemical drums lay scattered around as did the occasional shell of a car picked cleaned of parts, like the carcass of a dead animal. Mounds of illegally-tipped waste helped to give the bleak decaying landscape an undulating character.

Up ahead he saw the perfect resting place. The enclosure—provided by several high mounds of dumped rubble — would provide perfect cover for the Sierra. He turned the car left and switched off the engine.

The perspex number plates offered little resistance to the screwdriver's blade as he ripped them off front and rear. Several lumps of concrete made suitable tools for shattering the windows of the car.

When he was satisfied, he opened the back and took out the petrol container. He doused every surface with the container's contents, giving special attention to the passenger seat, where the broken number plates sat. When all the liquid was used up he threw the empty receptacle on the back seat.

From his pocket he took a handkerchief-sized piece of rag and wiped it in some of the petrol on the dashboard. As he walked away to implement the final part of the operation a thought crossed his mind. He strolled back to the car, opened the driver's door and ejected the cassette. It would be a shame to lose that, he thought. He looked at the car's stereo for a moment. Yeah it was a nice sound system, pity. But that's the way it goes, he thought.

He wrapped a stone in the cloth and set the petrol-damp corner alight. From about about ten feet away he aimed the cloth at the hole where the rear window used to be. As soon as his hand released the projectile, he turned and started to run.

He could hear a loud 'whoosh' as the petrol ignited and he felt the flames' heat at the back of his head. He turned to see the car engulfed in a wall of orange flames. A dense cloud of black, foul-smelling smoke rose into the night sky. The brightness of the flames lit up the immediate area and the heat scorched the grass and weeds, even though they were wet from the night's dew.

The cop killer carried on running across the waste ground. After a few hundred yards he could no longer see the car, just the tips of the flames dancing at the top of the large rubble mounds. As he reached the road the loud 'boom' of the petrol tank igniting caused him to turn back and see a large mushroom of flame rise and then disappear into the night sky.

The waste ground was located in a section of the Grimthorpe Industrial Estate in north London. Lloyd had noticed the dumping ground about a month before when he dropped off a parcel for a printing company located on the estate. It was a good spot for car thieves to work undisturbed, stripping their booty. The nearest houses were over half a mile away.

As he walked in the cold night air he thought it a shame he'd had to torch the car. It had been a reliable work-horse over the past months and he had just set fire to sixteen hundred pounds worth of hard earned corn. Still, it was better he got rid of any potential evidence, he reasoned. It was a long and cold walk to Wood Green, but he thought it better to head in the direction of a place he knew, than wonder the unknown territory of north London.

It was 1:00am when he strolled into the mini cab office near Wood Green station and got a car. On the journey back to Bow he reflected on the previous night's liaison with Jackie Spencer. It had been a disaster. Not only did she know where he lived, but also knew who he was. He had taken a risk and all because he wanted to spend the night with her. Now his future lay in the hands of someone else who was a journalist and who he hardly knew. She had given her word not to reveal his identity in any feature she wrote, but could he really trust a journalist? What would she say when the police came to interview her after the world saw the story? How long would it take them to get the info out of her ? What's to say she would even stick to her word in the first place? He was caught between a rock and a hard place and wasn't sure what his next move should be. There was one piece of unfinished business he had to take care of and he would have to do it in the next few days. It was now Friday and he knew The Inquirer would be hitting the streets the next Wednesday. He didn't have much time.

Back at his yard, the cop killer sat on his bed, thinking out the runnings for the next few days. He felt like a trapped man with the hunters closing in on him. He kept cursing his mistake in inviting the journalist back to his place. He paced up and down the narrow confines of the bedroom, like a panther in a cage.

But two hours earlier he had felt like a free man, now he was here trying to flee the enclosing walls of his self-made prison.

He sat, paced and sat again for the next hour: thinking and rethinking until he conceded that it was a fruitless exercise. He might as well catch some sleep as mash up his head trying to sort out something that couldn't be fixed. He kicked off his shoes and lay down...

The man with the white shirt and tie showed him where the various switches were, and how the alarm

176

system worked. He handed the cop killer the keys and went back inside the office. The silver Ford Granada had a big luxury feel compared to his old Sierra and he felt good as he pulled out of Express Car Rentals and got onto the Stratford one-way system. He had hired it for a week; which would be enough time to get things sorted, he reckoned.

Heading back to Bow, he stopped at a telephone box to make a call. It was Friday 11:00am.

"Hello Jackie, it's me Lloyd... How's everything going? Did you have trouble from your boyfriend about the other night?"

"You told him what?"

"He believed a story as crazy as that...? Bwoy, you women are deadly. I've been warned. On a serious tip Jackie, I need to ask you a big favour... not to write any article about me and to destroy the letters I sent you and the bullet and driving license... No jus' hol' on Jackie. Let me finish, nuh man. If you print that article I'm done, finished. The police will be on your case and you'll have to tell them everything. I jus' have one piece ah business to sort out. If you print that story the radics will be on me from when the paper lands on the newsagent shelf... No Jackie, don't give me none of this shit that it's your job. You're free to do what you want. Let me ask you sump'n. Does anyone else know you met me...? There you have it. If yah editor nuh know, then the decision is yours. True...? No, no Jackie, the decision is yours. And yours alone. You don't haffe do nut'n."

The cop killer kept feeding coins into the slot as the telephone conversation carried on in a heated manner. After twenty minutes he felt it was pointless trying to argue with her. She was still insisting on publishing the piece. He slammed the phone down and kicked open the door. Scowling at the annoyed queue of people waiting outside the box, he stormed back to the car and aggressively cut into the traffic, nearly causing an accident in the process...

The clump of trees provided a much needed shelter from the piercing December wind which blew unchecked across the open expanse of heath land. The cop killer jogged on the spot to keep his limbs warm and pulled his black woollen ski hat down over his ears. A track suit was not the most effective clothing for keeping out the cold but it meant that a man running at night would receive less attention from passers by.

Despite the cold, the cop killer was grateful to the weather. This had been the first night since Friday when it had not poured down with rain. He had spent three miserable wet nights under those trees, hoping for a sighting of his elusive prey. His late evening vigils had been in vain; the beast did not show itself.

Located near to the top of the Leytonstone High Road, Whipps Cross Common with its large lake was a popular spot with joggers, anglers, and shagging couples during the summer months. Now, in the nearing depths of winter, only the die-hards ventured onto the common. The cop killer knew the habits of of his chosen prey well. He had spent several evenings watching in the shadows. He patiently waited until he was ready to strike. With his impending exposure in The Inquirer he had been forced to act sooner than he had wanted. He hoped he had sussed the routine of his target carefully. He checked his watch; it was 9:30 pm. If there was going to be a showing, he reasoned, then it would surely happen soon. He checked he was ready, and whether the area was free of people.

Fifteen minutes later his waiting paid off. He prepared himself. The target was as regular as clock-work and running in the same clothes and along the same route as

178

usual. He was getting closer and the cop killer made his final preparations checking that the coast was clear.

"Here we go." He whispered to himself as the jogger passed the clump of trees.

As soon as the man had jogged about ten yards past the trees, the cop killer set off like the final runner in a relay race. His baton, however, was of a heavier and more deadly construction. He was upon his prey and the jogger didn't even know it. His progress had been swift but silent. The jogger didn't know what hit him.

Like a hunter culling a seal, the cop killer swung the improvised, lead cosh with the required amount of force. It hit near to the side of the jogger's head and sent him crashing to the ground.

Lying face down, the man tried to crawl up onto his feet, but the cop killer was already on his prey. A metre length of thin nylon rope was quickly pulled out of the cop killer's pocket and tied around his victim's neck. He pulled with all his might on each end of the rope. His right knee pressed down hard at the top of the man's back. The cop killer pulled, then released, to catch his breath before doing it again. The cop killer was gulping for air and his mouth was dry. He wasn't sure how long he pulled on the rope but it seemed like a long time. Then the body of the jogger was totally still.

It was too dark to see clearly whether the blow from the lead bar had cut his victim's skin. The cop killer had tried to apply enough force to bring him down, but not leave any evidence of an attack. With Sergeant Summers boo-yakkad and now Inspector Reid eradicated, even a half-wit cop would suspect the connection and pay Lloyd and his brother a visit. The infamous past mistake of the Inspector would be well remembered by those in and out of the Met. With no body or evidence of a murder, they could'nt pin anything on him or Phillip. It was now of course all pointless, because of the story in tomorrow's

Inquirer. But he'd planned it this way, and he would follow out his plans to the letter.

There was no one in sight, so he took his chance to heave the body of the Inspector onto his shoulders and carry it through the trees to where the Ford Granada was parked. He dumped the body in the boot and chucked in the incriminating lead pipe. After checking he'd left no obvious clues at the scene of the attack, he set off in the Granada.

It felt like one of the last pieces of a jigsaw had been put in its place. The three people who had been mainly responsible for his mother's death had been eliminated and in his own way he had brought to her, in death, the justice she had been denied when alive. He blamed the Sergeant and the Inspector, but he also blamed the whole system. It was one big rotten apple with lots of gnawing maggots burrowing away inside. He would have liked to have taken them all on but he only had one gun and not a whole heap of ammo. There were times when he told himself that he would carry on the fight until the radics dropped him with a sniper's rifle, but the other side of him was tired of the struggle; tired of the war. The anger that had driven him on was growing weaker by the day and he didn't have the will to carry on. Sooner or later, he reasoned, even the most dedicated soldier must come home from the war.

Life was becoming more of a struggle everyday and he wasn't sure he could keep on going. The daily existence in the urban jungle was driving him mad. It had got him so crazy that he didn't give a second thought to blowing some small-time drugs pusher away, or breaking the legs of just another out of control rude bwoy. Everything seemed to be getting confused again. He wasn't sure what was the right way or if there was a point in going anyway. A few months ago it had seemed as clear as day what he had to do, now it was getting out of focus again.

It would be the start of the end tomorrow, he had taken a journey down that wild and twisting path; now it looked as though he'd run out of road.

Fuck. He never did get his will sorted out like he said he would. Maybe he could do it himself on a bit of paper. Yeah, maybe that would be legally okay. He had the money in the bank and that was about it. There wasn't much else. A hi-fi, some tapes, a few books, and about an eighth of some particularly good herb. That was it. Not a whole heap of things to worry about...

'Beeeeep', 'beeeeep'.

He looked up at the green traffic light and suddenly realised that the horns were for his benefit. He pushed his foot on the speedo and shot off down the North Circular Road. He couldn't remember driving there; he'd been so wrapped up in his thoughts.

He wasn't far away now from the Inspector's final burial place, on the same ground where he'd laid the Sierra to rest. It somehow seemed fitting that the two pieces of the puzzle should end up in the same place.

He turned off the North Circular Road and headed in the direction of the Grimthorpe Industrial Estate. He drove to the planned spot and parked the car. He turned off the lights.

The memory of two nights ago came back to him. It had been pouring with rain at the time; totally pissing down. He remembered the rain soaking through his clothes as he worked the shovel. Four hours non stop rapid back-breaking work. He looked at the blisters on his hands as if he needed some physical evidence to remind him. God that was hard work! Damn hard work.

He got out of the car and walked over to his labour of hate. The planks of wood were still there, covered over with rubbish to hide them. He pulled away the

camouflage and removed the planks. A neatly dug hole
about four feet deep by a yard wide was the fruits of his
hours of hard work the other night. Now it was time to
bury the past.

He opened the car's boot. He staggered back and
couldn't understand why his vision was blurred. Oh the
pain. As he stumbled away he felt another blow on his
shoulder. As his senses started to override the concussion,
he realised what was happening. The 'dead man' in the
boot was attacking him with the lead pipe he had not
long used on the man. Jesus Christ he wasn't dead — he
wasn't fucking dead!

The cop killer wanted to get away and regain his
senses before dealing with the man. The Inspector wasn't
going to give him that luxury. The cop killer couldn't
seem to see properly but he could make out the shape
coming towards him. He started to run as best as he
could. His hand rubbed his eye and he realised why his
vision was blurred. The gash above his right eyebrow was
oozing blood down into his eye. He wiped again and his
vision was much better.

The lead pipe blow to his right leg sent him sprawling
into the muddy ground, but he couldn't lie there. He
scrambled to his feet to run again but the blow to his back
brought him down again. He was lying face down in the
mud and trying to turn over.

'Thump'. He was glad it had missed his head. But the
pain in his shoulder was of limited consolation. He
turned over to see the Inspector raise the pipe above his
head and bring it down with great force. The cop killer
guessed right and turned his head to the left. The pipe
thudded into the soft ground.

The cop killer took his chance. He kicked and swung
his leg round in an arc, catching The Inspector at the back
of his left ankle sufficiently to make his leg slide from
under him on the slippery muddy ground.

He took his chance to get up and start to carry his injured body as quickly as was possible. If only he could get back to the car. He tried to get his bearings together but there wasn't time. He could hear the angry curses of the Inspector close behind him.

"Where's you fucking going, nigga? Come here you cunt."

"I ain't finished with you yet. You black bastard!"

The Inspector's voice was shaking with a crazed anger and the cop killer realised if he didn't move himself he would become the dead prey. He turned and saw the buildings of the Industrial Estate to his right. That's where the car was parked and that's where he needed to be. It would mean running in the direction of The Inspector, but that was his only way out. He turned and bolted to the right. The Inspector saw the move and ran to try and cut off the cop killer's escape.

They both ran as quickly as they could. The cop killer saw that he was not going to get to the road before the Inspector, but he hoped his momentum would carry him through the danger zone. As he got near to the Inspector he raised his arms up around his face to protect himself.

One blow struck his forearm and nearly knocked him over but he kept going. In his desperation the Inspector hurled the pipe at his target. It missed, whistling over the head of the cop killer.

The cop killer was nearly on home base when disaster struck. His muddy shoes lost their grip at the crucial moment and he slipped onto his hands and knees. It was enough time for the Inspector to gain sufficient ground. The cop moved with speed and brought his foot up into the ribs of the cop killer as he struggled to get upright. The blow winded him and it was followed by several more.

The cop killer tried staggering on and made it to the road and within half a dozen feet of the car. The fists of the Inspector rained down on him but he keep going. He was now against the side of the car, taking blows to his face, stomach and chest. The winding left him weak and gulping for breath. He didn't know how much more of this beating he could take. He fought to remain conscious and hoped that he would get a chance. It came quicker than he thought. The Inspector ran out of steam and stopped to gulp a breath of air. It was his only chance. Before the cop could resume, the cop killer punched the man's face with all the energy he had left in his aching right arm. The blow had the desired effect. It knocked the man back sufficiently for the cop killer to open the driver's door and get in the car. He slammed the door and pressed down the door lock. It was to be only a short rest. He saw the Inspector's hand with the brick and closed his eyes to prevent the shower of glass from blinding him.

"No fucking car door is gonna stop me nigga?"

The Inspector reached in and pulled up the door lock. He opened the door ready to finish off the 'black bastard'.

"Fuck you nigga!" he seethed.

"Fuck you pig!" were the last words the Inspector heard.

The .45 blasted him in the chest, sending him slumping to his knees. The second bullet burst straight through his head, taking a large piece of his brain with it. With his hand on the pump, the cop killer blasted bullet after bullet into the limp body of the Inspector. The big bore blaster finally ran out of shells and he dropped the gun.

Half an hour passed before the cop killer had regained enough energy to finish off what needed to be done. It took another hour of shovelling to fill up the cop's grave and properly cover over and camouflage the area.

He put the Granada in gear and headed north-eastwards, with the cold wind blowing in through the smashed driver's door glass.

FOURTEEN

The blaring horn of a tug boat woke him from his sleep. It was almost light and a cold wind from the Thames rattled the loose planks of wood in the old riverside warehouse. It was a part of Woolwich too run down and industrial to attract the trendy riverside property developers, and one of the last real pieces of riverside land still untouched by the hand of 'progress'.

It was a place Lloyd often used to retreat to when he sought solace; a place to go and meditate and reason. Now this was the end of the road. He felt bruised and battered, both in his body and in his mind.

He got out of the car and stepped into the bracing cold of that new December day, heading towards the edge of the river. He stopped to watch a Norwegian Vessel carrying timber head up the river. At least it wasn't fucking raining, he told himself. He pulled the empty magazine from his 'matic and hurled it into the choppy river waters, inserted a fresh clip into the Colt and pulled back the slide. Loaded and ready for action.

As he stood there, the snap-shot images of his journey down the highway to hell flashed in his head. The cop crashing on his bike; 'Cockney Wanker' taking it in the gut; Michael Watts' face; the Inspector; the concrete falling onto the cop in Stockwell — hosts of fleeting images flicking through his mind like a slide projector going at double time.

He raised the gun to the side of his head and his finger reached for the trigger. He ordered his finger to end it all now, but the shaking hand didn't want to.

His hand dropped to his side. His mouth blew hard.

He wiped the sweat from his brow. He brought his hand back and hurled the gun into the air. As if in slow motion, it rose high in the air and then started its descent to earth, spinning like a steel boomerang. It landed with a 'splash' and disappeared into the depths of the river.

Lloyd got in the car and headed for Bow. The roads were quiet at that time of the morning as he headed back to the flat. He stopped on the way to pick up a copy of The Inquirer.

His body hurt like fuck and he felt worn and weary. In a bathrobe and with a cup of coffee in hand, he flicked through The Inquirer. It was only after he looked carefully for the fourth time that it slowly dawned on him that the article wasn't in there. Absolutely nothing.

In his glass-walled sanctum Inquirer Editor Wesley Banfield was reading the letter again in disbelief.

Dear Wesley,

I write to let you know that I am resigning from my post as reporter at The Inquirer. I don't really think the world of journalism is right for me and I don't want to become what it seems one has to be to get on..."

He kept reading the letter, trying to make sense of why one of his most promising reporters was packing it all in...

Back in his Bow flat, Lloyd felt like he had been given a new lease of life. He lay in the bath, smoking a spliff and wearily smiled to himself.

EPILOGUE

Lloyd Baker was questioned in connection with the murders of four police officers. No charges were brought due to lack of evidence. He moved to west London where he presently works as a minicab driver.

SKANK

Pure Ragga!

*The slackest magazine....*Out April '94

Comic Genius

Ragga culture is here to stay and a new comic *Skank*. shortly due for publication by X Press. the radical black publishing house. is a reflection of that junglist vibe. *Skank* is the brain child of Lewisham-born Bobby Joseph. aided and abetted by fellow cartoonist Gee Ma~ photographer A~